the
Lucent
Library
of
Historical
Eras

Elizabethan England

Great Elizabethan Playwrights

Other titles in the Lucent Library of Historical Eras, Elizabethan England, include:

Elizabeth I and Her Court
A History of the Elizabethan Theater
Life in Elizabethan London
Primary Sources

The Lucent Library of Historical Eras

Elizabethan England

Great Elizabethan Playwrights

Don Nardo

LUCENT BOOKS®

THOMSON

GALE

San Diego • Detroit • New York • San Francisco • Cleveland • New Haven, Conn. • Waterville, Maine • London • Munich

THOMSON
———⋆———™
GALE

*On cover: Revered playwright William
Shakespeare is pictured in his thirties.*

© 2003 by Lucent Books. Lucent Books is an imprint of The Gale Group, Inc.,
a division of Thomson Learning, Inc.

Lucent Books® and Thomson Learning™ are trademarks used herein under license.

For more information, contact
Lucent Books
27500 Drake Rd.
Farmington Hills, MI 48331-3535
Or you can visit our Internet site at http://www.gale.com

LIBRARY OF CONGRESS CATALOGING-IN-PUBLICATION DATA

Nardo, Don, 1947–
    Great Elizabethan playwrights / by Don Nardo.
p. cm. — (The Lucent library of historical eras: Elizabethan England)
Includes bibliographical references and index.
Summary: Discusses the origins of English-speaking theater and includes facts about
seven early Elizabethan playwrights, including William Shakespeare.
    ISBN 1-59018-017-8 (hardback : alk. paper)
    1. English drama—Early modern and Elizabethan, 1500–1600—History and criti-
cism—Juvenile literature. 2. Dramatists, English—early modern, 1500–1700—
Biography—Juvenile literature. 3. Theater—England—History—16th century—Juvenile
literature. 4. Shakespeare, William, 1564–1616—Juvenile literature. [1. English drama—
Early modern and Elizabethan, 1500–1600—History and criticism. 2. Dramatists,
English. 3. Theater—England—History—16th century. 4. Shakespeare, William,
1564–1616.] I. Title. II. Lucent library of historical eras. Elizabethan England.
    PR421 .N37 2003
    822′ .309—dc21

2001006602

Printed in the United States of America

Contents

Foreword

Looking back from the vantage point of the present, history can be viewed as a myriad of intertwining roads paved by human events. Some paths stand out—broad highways whose mileposts, even from a distance of centuries, are clear. The events that propelled the rise to power of Germany's Third Reich, its role in World War II, and its eventual demise, for example, are well defined and documented.

Other roads are less distinct, their route sometimes hidden from view. Modern legislatures may have developed from old tribal councils, for example, but the links between them are indistinct in places, open to discussion and interpretation.

The architecture of civilization—law, religion, art, science, and government—as well as the more everyday aspects of our culture—what we eat, what we wear—all developed along the historical roads and byways. In that progression can be traced every facet of modern life.

A broad look back along these roads reveals that many paths—though of vastly different character—seem to converge at a few critical junctions. These intersections are those great historical eras that echo over the long, steady course of human history, extending beyond the past and into the present.

These epic periods of time are the focus of Lucent's Library of Historical Eras. They shine through the mists of history like beacons, illuminated by a burst of creativity that propels events forward—so bright that we, from thousands of years away, can clearly see the chain of events leading to the present.

Each Lucent Library of Historical Eras consists of a set of books that highlight various aspects of these major eras. For example, the Elizabethan England library features volumes on Queen Elizabeth I and her court, Elizabethan theater, the great playwrights, and everyday life in Elizabethan London.

The mini-library approach allows for the division of each era into its most significant and most interesting parts and the exploration of those parts in depth. Also, social and cultural trends as well as illustrative documents and eyewitness accounts can be prominently featured in individual volumes.

Lucent's Library of Historical Eras presents a wealth of information to young readers. The lively narrative, fully documented primary and secondary source quotations, maps, photographs, sidebars, and annotated bibliographies serve as launching points for class discussion and further research.

In studying the great historical eras, students also develop a better understanding of our own times. What we learn from the past and how we apply it in the present may shape the future and may determine whether our era will be a guiding light to those traveling future roads.

Introduction:
Birth of the English-Speaking Theater

Today, people in the United States, Britain, Canada, Australia, and other English-speaking countries take for granted the existence of popular plays, movies, and television shows. The word "popular" is used here in its purest sense; that is, it denotes drama that aims at, is easily understood by, and appeals to the masses, including people of all walks of life. Essential to this widespread appeal, of course, is the fact that the actors speak plain English; and therefore their words and ideas are readily understood. Here again, everyone simply takes for granted that the English language is rich and sophisticated enough to translate the wide array of human emotions and ideas depicted in drama.

This situation is relatively new, however. As late as the early 1500s, widely popular drama written in English did not yet exist. It was created in an amazingly short time span by the dramatists of the Elizabethan Age (the period in England lasting from the mid-1500s to the early 1600s). Actors had performed plays in England before the Elizabethans. But no public theaters had been built yet; and

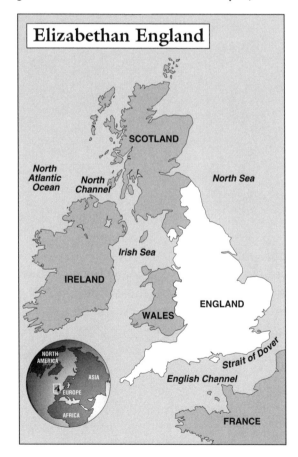

Elizabethan England

the pre-Elizabethan plays were written for specific and limited audiences, including church congregations, schoolboys, or nobles and their courtiers. Moreover, many such plays were written in Latin, since English was still considered too vulgar. And those plays that *were* composed in English tended to be simplistic, unsophisticated, and uninventive and featured guttural, often obscene dialogue.

All of this changed when the Elizabethan playwrights came on the scene. The greatest and most influential of the Elizabethan pioneers were John Lyly (born in 1554), Thomas Kyd (ca. 1558), George Peele (ca. 1556), Robert Greene (ca. 1558), Christopher Marlowe (1564), William Shakespeare (1564), and Ben Jonson (1572). Perhaps their chief hallmarks

This modern sketch of an Elizabethan playhouse shows that spectators both sat in seats and stood on the ground.

were inventiveness and boldness. Yet they did not simply throw out all that had come before and start anew. Instead, they took the strongest, most effective elements of older forms of theater and drama and combined them to create fresh, new forms. Furthermore, they crafted their works in English verse and prose that was both sophisticated and beautiful; and they presented them in buildings constructed specifically for plays—the first theaters in the English-speaking world.

It is important to emphasize that these playwrights did not get together in a concerted effort to create a new form of drama. Indeed, as former Princeton University scholar Thomas M. Parrott puts it, "Each was an individual genius and contributed something of his own to the popular stage; there is a vast difference between the courtly comedies of Lyly and the heroic tragedies of Marlowe."[1] Yet certain vital similarities exist in all of the Elizabethan dramatists, qualities that unify them and their works in very real ways. "They were all born poets," says Parrott,

> makers, inventors; not one of them was content to follow the beaten path of traditional drama. They were all artists in words, consciously engaged in devising for the drama a better medium of expression than it had hitherto [previously] possessed. They were all imbued with the spirit of romance, seekers after the strange and lovers of beauty.[2]

Another important trait the Elizabethan playwrights had in common was a sense of life and humanity they shared with their audiences. Though they were a good deal more educated than the average person, they were not rich, snooty intellectuals living and writing in ivory towers far removed from everyday life. In fact, most were active members of the very public for which they wrote, men about town who regularly patronized taverns and knew what it was like to struggle for a living. Their great achievement was to use their superior educations and inborn talents to guide and shape public tastes, to give everyday people of all classes entertainment of a scale and quality they had never known before. And in so doing, they created the English-speaking theater practically overnight.

"On Your Imaginary Forces Work": The Elizabethan Theater

To an enormous degree, the Elizabethan playwrights helped to define and at the same time were themselves defined by the historical age in which they lived. They came into the world at a particularly crucial historical time—the last half of the sixteenth century. And their birthplace was then one of the world's most pivotal nations—England. The era in question is usually referred to as the Elizabethan Age because it roughly encompassed the pivotal and fruitful forty-five-year reign (1558–1603) of one of England's greatest rulers, Elizabeth I.

As it happened, this was one of the richest, most dynamic, and most opportune cultural and professional settings for aspiring poets and dramatists in all of Western history. Numerous great or highly influential writers were born within a dozen years of the greatest of their number—William Shakespeare (1564)—and published works during his lifetime. These included Francis Bacon, Thomas Kyd, Thomas Nashe, Robert Greene, Christopher Marlowe, Ben Jonson, and John Donne, among many others.

The Medieval World Transformed

Moreover, these writers were born in a time when powerful European nations like England were greatly expanding their horizons. It was "an era of change and

Queen Elizabeth I in the early years of her reign. The era in which she ruled came to bear her name.

The gradual break-up of feudalism [the system in which powerful lords exploited the labor of agricultural serfs] . . . the discovery of gunpowder and . . . the mariner's compass and the possibility of safely navigating the limitless ocean, the production of paper and the invention of printing, and . . . the Copernican system of astronomy which formulated a new center of the universe—all of these new conceptions had a profound effect upon human thought and became the foundations for intellectual, moral, social, and economic changes which quickly made themselves felt.[3]

In addition to these forces that shaped Europe in the 1500s, several important events took place in England during Shakespeare's, Marlowe's, and Jonson's own lifetimes. Perhaps the most renowned of these—the English defeat of the huge Spanish Armada (an event that saved England from invasion and foreign occupation)—occurred in 1588. Not long afterward, Sir Francis Drake, Sir John Hawkins, and other adventurous English sea captains helped to turn the sea lanes into great highways for England's growing naval power. And in 1607, when Shakespeare was about forty-three and Jonson about thirty-four, English settlers founded the colony of Jamestown in

restlessness," remarks Shakespearean scholar Karl Holzknecht.

Everywhere—in religion, in philosophy, in politics, in science, in literature—new ideas were springing into life and coming into conflict with the established order of things. . . . A whole series of events and discoveries, coming together at the end of the fifteenth century [just preceding the Elizabethan Age], transformed . . . many of the institutions and the habits of mind that we call medieval.

Virginia, giving England a foothold in the New World.

England's command of the waves brought it commercial success, and its ports and towns became rapidly expanding centers of high finance, social life, and the arts. The nation's chief city, London, grew from a town of fifty thousand inhabitants in 1520 to a true city of more than two hundred thousand in 1600—a phenomenal rate of growth. Elizabethan playwright Thomas Dekker (born about 1572) described the hustle and bustle that was at the time quite new to London:

In every street, carts and coaches make such a thundering as if the world ran upon wheels. At every corner, men, women, and children meet in such shoals [close-packed groups] that posts are set up . . . to strengthen the houses, lest with jostling one another they should shoulder them down. Besides, hammers are beating in one place, tubs hooping [barrels being bound] in another, pots clinking in a third, water tankards running at a tilt in a fourth. Here are porters sweating under burdens, their merchant's men bearing bags of money. [Peddlers] . . . skip out of one shop into another. Tradesmen . . . are lusty at legs [swift] and never stand still.[4]

The Spanish Armada threatens England. The defeat of the Armada helped to establish Elizabethan England as a leading naval power.

13

Amid all of this social and commercial hubbub, the theater, increasingly recognized as an art form, provided a fertile creative atmosphere for the efforts and innovations of ambitious young playwrights like Dekker, Greene, Kyd, Marlowe, and Shakespeare.

Building on the Past

Though the bustling, creative setting in which these and other Elizabethan dramatists worked was a new phenomenon and they were highly inventive writers, they were very much influenced by past theatrical genres and styles. And their works built directly on plays composed and performed in England in the prior two centuries. In the late Middle Ages, beginning about 1300, mummers had come into fashion. These were masked persons who performed at local festivals and celebrations, such as

A group of mummers dressed as animals entertains at a party held in an English tavern.

weddings, religious holidays, May Day observances, and so forth; they put on skits in which they did not speak (hence their name, from "mum," meaning silent), but rather pantomimed simple stories.

Also in the fourteenth century, another kind of performance—the "miracle play"—came into vogue. Written by priests and schoolmasters, these short, simple works were staged in churches during Sunday services and reenacted miraculous passages from the Bible.

Unlike the mummers, actors in the miracle plays did speak. Their dialogue usually consisted of close paraphrases of biblical lines. For example, one popular play, performed on Easter Sunday, reenacted the visit of three women to Christ's tomb after his resurrection. The women encountered an angel at the tomb and told him they were seeking Jesus of Nazareth, and he replied that Jesus had risen. The miracle plays were in Latin, the formal language of the Church. They were eventually staged outdoors and became quite large-scale, sometimes with dozens or even hundreds of players and elaborate sets and costumes.

In the fifteenth century, the Church came to have less control over play presentation. Though miracle plays were still performed, another genre—the "morality play"—evolved from them. Morality plays had worldly settings and dealt with stories of good and evil as these concepts related to real-life people. Some of the characters were still biblical—for instance, Eve, Noah, Abraham, and so on—but other common ones included Beauty, Knowledge, Fellowship, and other "truths" of the human condition, who interacted to teach the audience a moral lesson.

Like the miracle plays, the morality plays rapidly became large-scale and required the services of many actors, costumers, and others. For a long time, these people were amateurs who played their various parts in the productions and then went back to their regular jobs in villages and towns. On the one hand, some of these people developed special theatrical skills, which they often passed on to their children; on the other, some found themselves "bitten by the acting bug," as people today refer to falling in love with the theater.

"Strolling" Professional Actors

As a result, as the sixteenth century dawned, a number of such amateurs

This sixteenth-century painting shows the background setting for an English miracle play entitled The Passion and Resurrection of Our Savior and Redeemer Jesus Christ.

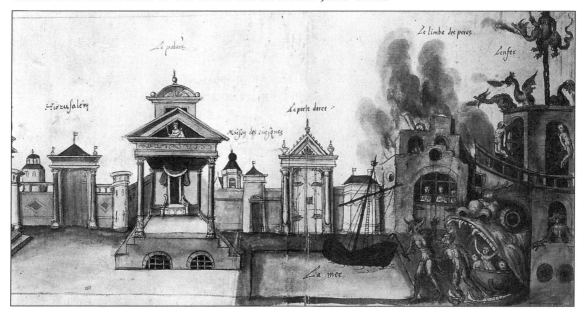

decided to try to actually earn a living by putting on plays. These first theatrical professionals became known as "strolling players" because they walked from place to place to put on their shows. Often jugglers, acrobats, singers, and dancers, as well as actors, they typically banded together into touring companies, carrying along their costumes and props. With names like the Queen's Men and the Earl of Worcester's Men, these companies presented the most popular plays of the day on makeshift wooden stages because no permanent theaters yet existed in England. Noted scholar A.A. Mendilow explains:

> All stage performances for public entertainment in the larger towns before and [in many cases] even after 1576 were conducted on movable platforms . . . covering a curtained lower story where the actors could change their costumes; the entry from below to the upper acting area could also serve as a "hellmouth" into which the wicked were thrown in the old religious drama. The platform was open on all four sides as a rule, and perhaps had a canopy against the rain. . . . The whole cart was on wheels and constituted a traveling theater which could be set up in market squares and open spaces. In Shakespeare's time, companies of actors still traveled in the provinces, especially when performances were forbidden

in London because of an outbreak of the plague.[5]

These roving players became extremely popular and came to draw large audiences, especially in the larger towns. Local innkeepers were quick to take note that business increased markedly when an acting company was in town. So, many innkeepers began offering their "inn yards," the open courtyards in the center of their U-shaped, multistoried establishments, as places for the actors to perform. A group of players would set up a temporary wooden stage in the yard. Some spectators stood on the ground around the stage, while others stood or sat in the tiered walkways that ran in front of the doors leading to the inn's rooms. Because the inns were often two or more stories high, these spectators looked down on the stage from above and therefore had excellent views of the action. The shape and features of inns and inn yards would later have a crucial influence on the structural design of the first English theaters.

As might be expected, the plays performed in town squares and inn yards attracted people of all walks of life, including poor and illiterate people. Traveling actors also performed in somewhat more refined venues, including the "great halls" of noblemen's houses and respectable colleges such as those at Oxford and Cambridge. In these indoor settings, the actors erected a large screen in the back of the room; the front of the

An engraving depicts a performance of Shakespeare's As You Like It *in an inn yard about 1600. Inn yards continued to present plays even after the first theaters were built.*

screen acted as a backdrop for the play's action, and behind it the actors changed their costumes and prepared to make their entrances.

The First Theaters

Not surprisingly, fast-growing London became the biggest magnet for strolling acting companies, since the city had the largest potential audience in the country. Reception was often mixed, however, not only in London but in other large towns as well. Many people flocked to see the plays whenever they could; but some city fathers and other upper-class individuals, especially churchmen, frowned on strolling actors,

seeing them as low-class tramps; and they sometimes refused to allow the players to stage their entertainments.

This situation changed when Queen Elizabeth came to power in the late 1550s. Elizabeth greatly enjoyed watching plays and encouraged their production, giving the infant English theater its single most significant boost. Demand for new plays and the new acting companies to perform them increased markedly. And in turn, the need was created for more fixed and permanent acting companies that could stay in London year-round and meet the demands of the quickly growing theatergoing public.

It soon became apparent that permanent acting companies required more permanent, formalized, and specialized structures to house them—in short, true theaters. In 1576, former actor and carpenter James Burbage erected the first theater in the English-speaking world. Appropriately called simply The Theatre, it stood in an open area in Shoreditch, north of the Thames River on the eastern edge of London. Recalling the effective theatrical setting of the inn yards, Burbage designed the structure to look something like a large inn yard. (Its exact features are unknown, but some surviving documents from that era suggest that it was round and that its stage was surrounded by three tiered galleries for the spectators.) In a sense, then, The Theatre was an inn yard without the inn around it.

The Theatre proved to be so popular that other businessmen began building theaters of their own. In 1577, only a year after Burbage constructed his theater, Henry Lanman opened The Curtain a short distance to the south. Next came The Rose, built in 1587 at Bankside, on the south side of the Thames, which soon became London's long-entrenched theater district. To the west of The Rose, a goldsmith named Francis Langley erected The Swan in 1595; and to the east of The Rose, a group of actors, among their number William Shakespeare, built The Globe in 1599. These men entered into a joint ownership deal with Sir Nicholas Brend, who owned the property, marking the first known instance in theatrical history of actors owning the theater in which they performed. A large proportion of the materials used in The Globe's construction came from The Theatre, which was dismantled in 1597 by James Burbage's sons—Richard and Cuthbert—after their lease ran out. Soon afterward came The Fortune, built in 1600 on London's north side, and the nearby Red Bull, erected in 1606.

Structure and Layout

Because all of these principal Elizabethan theaters long ago ceased to exist, their exact layouts and features are somewhat uncertain. However, as pointed out by Michael Hattaway, a noted scholar of Elizabethan drama:

> Evidence suggests that their external structure and internal layout were broadly similar. The Globe, after all, was built with the same timbers as the Theatre, and the Fortune contract specified that although the auditorium was to be square, the stage was to be modeled on that of the Globe. Both the Globe and the Fortune were built by the same builder, Peter Street. . . . And we know the stage [of The Globe] was modeled on that of the Swan.[6]

Luckily, an extremely important piece of evidence for the structure of the Elizabethan playhouses was discovered in 1880. Consisting of a drawing made of the interior of The Swan in 1596 by a

Dutch visitor, Johan de Witt, the sketch shows a round, open structure with a large, flat, raised stage in the middle. Behind the stage rises a two-story structure—the "tiring house"; equipped with doors, it appears to be a more elaborate and permanent version of the screens used by the actors who performed in the great halls. And projecting outward from the sides of the tiring house are the galleries for the spectators, in the manner of English inn yards. Based on this and other evidence, much of it from the plays of the era, most modern experts believe that Shakespeare's Globe possessed roughly the same features, as summarized here in more detail by Shakespearean scholar Ronald Watkins:

The [building's] octagonal frame is about 84 feet in outside diameter—hardly more than the length of a lawn-tennis court. A concentric octagon within the frame bounds the Yard, which is open to the sky. Between the two octagons the space is roofed and the building rises to three stories. Nearly five of the eight sides of the octagonal frame are occupied by galleries from which the eyes of the spectators converge upon the stage. The Yard will hold 600 standing close-packed (the groundlings); the three galleries about 1,400. . . . Intimacy

[between actors and audience] is possible at the Globe because of the position of the Platform [i.e., the stage]. The middle point of the front edge is the exact center of the octagon. The actor . . . can have his audience on three sides of him. There is real distance in the depth of the stage, and an actor in the Study [or discovery space, the small area, often curtained, at the rear of the stage] will seem remote while another in

Dutchman Johan de Witt's famous 1596 sketch of the inside of London's Swan theater.

19

front seems close at hand; this contrast in their relation to the audience is often used for dramatic purpose. The Platform is the main field of action for the players. . . . It tapers towards the front, stands probably between 4 and 5 feet from the floor of the Yard, and is protected from the groundlings by rails; the front edge is 24 feet wide, at its widest it is 41 feet; its depth from front to Study-curtain is 29 feet; and the Study

An old drawing shows The Globe, built by a group of actors, among them William Shakespeare.

itself, when open, adds a further 7 or 8 feet. Conspicuous towards the front of the Platform stand the two pillars supporting the . . . Heavens [a rooflike canopy overhanging the middle of the stage]. . . . The tiring-house [containing dressing rooms for the actors] is the permanent background to the platform; its back is turned to the afternoon sun, so that no freaks of light and shade distract from the illusion [since the plays were presented in the afternoon]. . . . On the Platform level the . . . Study is flanked by two doors . . . the two main entries for the players.[7]

Settings and Costumes

Because of the shape and nature of such theaters, certain theatrical conventions (common, accepted traditions and practices) developed. For example, the stage was open, bare, and surrounded by spectators on three sides, so there was little or nothing in the way of sets or painted backdrops. Neither were there programs to provide the spectators with background material and other explanations of the action. Accordingly, audiences were expected to use their imaginations to a much greater degree than theater-goers are today. Often, a short prologue spoken by one of the players set the scene. Perhaps the most famous example is the speech of the Chorus (a single actor) from the opening of Shakespeare's magnificent historical play, *Henry V.*

"Can this cockpit [circular structure] hold the vast fields of France?" the character asks the audience. "Or may we cram within this wooden O [another way of saying a circular structure] the very casques [helmets] that did affright the air at Agincourt [site of Henry's greatest military victory]?" Obviously, the small theater in question *cannot* hold entire battlefields and armies. So the Chorus admonishes the watchers:

On your imaginary forces work.

Suppose within the girdle of these walls

Are now confined two mighty monarchies [i.e., England and France]. . . .

Piece out our imperfections with your thoughts;

Into a thousand parts divide one man [i.e., imagine that one actor represents a thousand soldiers]. . . .

Think when we talk of horses, that you see them

Printing their proud hoofs in the receiving earth;

For 'tis your thoughts that now must deck [dress up] our kings.[8]

On the other hand, Elizabethan actors used many props (weapons, shovels and other tools, books and scrolls, musical instruments, chairs and other furniture, and so on) and sound effects from behind the stage (battle noises, court music, thun-

der, and the like). Also, costumes were often elaborate. (Apparently, though, they were not very historically accurate, the convention being to dress almost everyone in contemporary Elizabethan clothes, no matter what the age and setting portrayed in the play.) A surviving 1602 costume inventory lists "a scarlet cloak with embroidered gold laces, with gold buttons of the same down the sides," and "a scarlet cloak laid down with silver lace and silver buttons"[9]; and a Swiss traveler, Thomas Platter, recorded in 1599 after viewing a play: "The comedians are most expensively and elegantly appareled [dressed]."[10] In general, actors were costumed according to accepted stereotypes of the day—that is, kings and queens wore crowns and fine ceremonial dress; doctors, bright red gowns; lawyers, black robes; country bumpkins, tall boots; fools (court jesters), long coats of motley (multicolored patches); virgins, white gowns; shepherds, white coats; sailors, canvas suits; and ghosts, garments made of animal skins and hair.

Other Theatrical Conventions

The queens in their elaborate dresses, the virgins in their white gowns, and other female characters were also part of another common convention of Elizabethan theater; namely, young men, rather than women, played these roles. English society viewed it as improper for women to appear on the stage. So the acting companies turned to using boys with slight

No matter what the historical period portrayed in a play, Elizabethan actors typically wore contemporary clothing, as shown here.

figures and high voices, a practice that began in the early 1500s. Some theatrical groups were actually made up entirely of boy players, among them the Children of the Royal Chapel and the Boys of St. Paul's Choir. Beginning around age ten, these young men learned to walk and talk like women and to apply women's make-up and wigs, as well as to dance, sing, and fence (since they sometimes doubled in male roles). When a boy's voice began to change, he either moved up into adult roles or retired from acting. Some of Shakespeare's most famous and challeng-

ing female roles—including Juliet and her nurse (in *Romeo and Juliet*), Ophelia and Queen Gertrude (in *Hamlet*), and Cleopatra (in *Antony and Cleopatra*) were originally portrayed, apparently quite convincingly, by boys.

Another character convention was the widespread use of clowns of various types. These were sometimes classic court jesters, such as the fool in Shakespeare's *King Lear* and Touchstone in *As You Like It*; but they were also country bumpkins and other humorous, clumsy, silly, or witty characters. In serious plays, including tragedies, they provided comic relief or made pithy comments about the human condition (or sometimes both), perhaps the most memorable example being the gravediggers in Shakespeare's *Hamlet.* Once an actor established himself as a clown, he usually played little else. The first Elizabethan actor who became widely renowned for his clown roles was Richard Tarlton, who died in 1588. His wit was said to be so quick that he could easily outtalk and put down hecklers who shouted insults at him from the audience. (Sometimes this impromptu banter went too far and disrupted the play, as evidenced by this speech from *Hamlet,* in which the title character addresses a group of actors preparing a performance: "Let those that play your clowns speak no more than is set down [written] for them, for there will be some of them that will themselves laugh to set on [provoke] some quantity of barren spectators to laugh too."[11])

Of the many other conventions in Elizabethan theater, most plays had five acts, each broken down into a number of scenes, and had two to four plotlines running simultaneously. In Shakespeare's *King Lear,* for example, three separate main stories are skillfully interwoven—that of the title character; that of Edmund, bastard son of Lear's trusted friend Gloucester; and that of Gloucester's other son, Edgar. In addition, minor stories of other characters appear within these main plots. The stories converge at various points, especially at the end, which resolves all of them in a gut-wrenching climax.

Elizabethan playwrights also frequently used the device of the soliloquy. This is a speech delivered by an actor alone on stage who thinks aloud, revealing to the audience the character's inner emotions or future plans. The Elizabethans obviously did not have the benefit of electronic recording techniques that allow modern stage, film, and television actors to sit

This seventeenth-century drawing depicts the widely famous and popular comic actor Richard Tarlton.

unmoving and have the audience hear what they are thinking. So they had to resort to the stylistic and decidedly unrealistic soliloquy. Yet the device is often compelling, as well as useful, in its own right. Perhaps the most famous examples in all of English literature— Hamlet's soliloquies—are powerful, absorbing journeys into the character's psyche.

Still another convention of the era was the liberal depiction of and audi-

The great English actor Sir Laurence Olivier portrays Hamlet, a character known for his soliloquies.

ences' fascination for fighting, killing, and blood. In the finales of most of the tragedies, in fact, the stage is literally littered with bodies. "The Elizabethans loved horrors," wrote the late noted scholar G.B. Harrison.

> They thoroughly enjoyed the spectacle of an execution for high treason when the condemned man was first half-hanged, then cut down, disemboweled, and finally hacked to pieces as a warning to others. But as the supply of traitors was uncertain, the theaters catered to these gruesome tastes by giving realistic scenes of bloodshed.[12]

The Elizabethan Dramatists

None of these conventions, characters, and plays would have been possible, of course, without the playwrights who conceived them. These men who gave the audiences scenes of gore, romance, friendship, heroism, politics, humor, and the full spectrum of human emotions varied in both the quantity and quality of their output. They also varied widely in their backgrounds and lifestyles. The names of more than two hundred Elizabethan dramatists have survived, although little is known about most of them and many of their works are now lost. Evidence shows that some were "gentleman amateurs" who composed only one or two plays and did not attempt to make a living as playwrights, while others were full-time professionals

who wrote dozens of plays and became household names. Still others collaborated (worked together) in order to work faster, since the demand for new plays became huge and unrelenting. As one scholar puts it:

> More, more, more, was the cry, and there were the wretchedly underpaid quill-pushers, often working in partnerships of two, three, or four, to grind the stuff out and meet demand.[13]

The first truly influential and successful playwrights of the period became known as the "university wits," who more or less dominated the theater scene from about 1585 to 1595. The more prominent of their number included John Lyly, Thomas Lodge, Thomas Kyd, George Peele, Robert Greene, Thomas Nashe, and Christopher Marlowe. Most were university-educated writers who applied real literary skill and inventiveness to the genre; before them, most plays had usually lacked one or more of the elements of complexity, good construction, witty dialogue, and well-drawn characters. They developed a sound structure on which other dramatists could build. Some of the later Elizabethan playwrights, like Thomas Heywood and John Marston, were also university men. But several others, among them Thomas Dekker, William Shakespeare, and Ben Jonson, were not. Shakespeare and Jonson were among a small group of professional

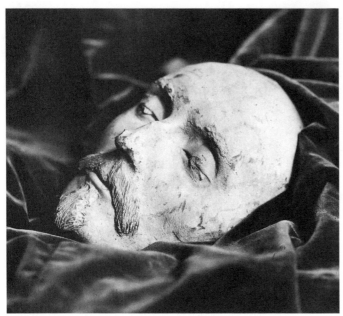

This death mask has been claimed by some to be that of the great Elizabethan playwright, William Shakespeare.

era (although Jonson and a few others were still working), and the English theater was clearly in decline. Under Elizabeth's successor, James I, the country's economy and prosperity suffered and the number of playgoers decreased. This in turn reduced demand for new plays. When James died in 1625, his son, Charles, ascended the throne. Then, in 1642, a civil war broke out and Parliament permanently closed the theaters. When they reopened under a new king in the 1660s, new styles of playwriting and play production came into fashion. Yet the influence of the Elizabethan dramatists—especially Marlowe, Shakespeare, and Jonson—remained powerful. Their strong sense of realism, rich characterization, soaring poetry, and pioneering work in theater design provided a foundation that has supported much of the English-speaking theater ever since.

actors who went on to become famous playwrights.

When Shakespeare died in 1616, he had already outlived Queen Elizabeth by thirteen years. He had also outlived most of the great actors and playwrights of the

The Courtly Dreamer: John Lyly

John Lyly was more than just the first of the Elizabethan university wits, that handful of highly educated writers who emerged on the English literary and theatrical scene in the 1580s. Modern scholars also credit Lyly with numerous other important firsts. He was among the first English writers to view prose (ordinary language, as opposed to poetic verses) as an artistic style; so he is often called one of the founders, if not *the* founder, of English prose writing. Lyly was also the author of the first novel written in the English language; the first truly professional English dramatist (his predecessors having been part-time amateurs); and the pioneer of the English comic play.

Students assigned to read Lyly's plays today are often surprised and disappointed by their loose structure and lack of strong characterization and robust humor and emotions. Certainly his plots, characters, and dialogue are rarely as developed and effective as those of later Elizabethan dramatists, especially Shakespeare and Jonson. One reason is that nearly all of Lyly's plays were performed in refined courtly settings, often before the queen herself; and accordingly, almost all are built around the theme of courtly love, which tended to be very mannered, polite, cool, and unemotional. Lyly's literary importance and popularity in his own day were based mainly on his use of the English language. As no one had before him, he made it sound beautiful and harmonious, and this had a strong influence on his successors, including Shakespeare. That Lyly's works seem lightweight and detached today may be attributed partly to the fact that they were, in retrospect, prototypes of the more substantial works of those successors. As Thomas Parrott puts it: "If today Lyly's [writing] seems outmoded, his wit thin, his frequent puns absurd, we should remember that [in his day] all this was new to the Elizabethan stage."[14]

Lyly's Oxford Years

Writing for the Elizabethan stage was not Lyly's sole achievement, however, as an examination of his fruitful but ultimately sad and unfulfilled life reveals. The exact details of his childhood are unknown, but the best scholarly estimate is that he was born at Canterbury, some fifty miles southeast of London, sometime between October 1553 and October 1554. The family had already achieved a fair amount of social distinction. Young John's father, Peter Lyly, was a clergyman at the famous Canterbury Cathedral. And his grandfather, William Lyly (or Lilly), was the author of the most widely used Latin grammar text of the era.

In 1569, when he was about sixteen, John Lyly entered Magdalen College (part of Oxford University), in Oxford, sixty miles northwest of London. He graduated from the school with an M.A. (Master of Arts) degree in 1575. Apparently his graduation brought relief to the faculty,

as some considerable circumstantial evidence suggests that Lyly was something of a disciplinary problem during his stay there. Gabriel Harvey, a noted Cambridge University scholar of that time, later made reference to the young man's "horning, gaming, fooling, and knaving"[15] at Oxford. And a long absence from school around 1570–1571 may have been the result of a suspension for bad behavior.

The events immediately following Lyly's graduation constitute more evidence that his schoolmasters were glad to be rid of him. The following year (1576), he decided he wanted to teach at Oxford, and realizing that the university officials would not be receptive, he wrote to a friend and wealthy patron, Lord Burleigh, asking him to go over their heads and petition the queen to get him a position. Apparently Burleigh felt such a request put him in too awkward a position, and Lyly's petition failed. In a huff, the young man left Oxford owing the university money for food consumed while at school and vowing to get even with the academics who disliked him.

The Invention of Euphuism

Lyly's revenge was not long in coming and took the form of one of the most important and influential English literary works created up to the time. In 1578, he published his widely popular *Euphues: The Anatomy of a Wit*, now seen as the first English novel. The simple plot revolves around the character Euphues, a

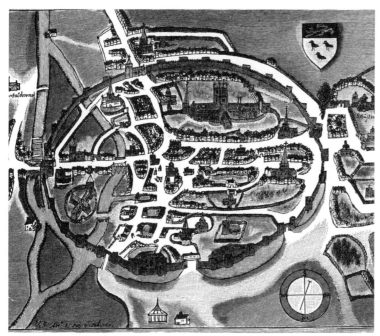

A seventeenth-century engraving shows Canterbury, the town where John Lyly was born.

It was not the book's approach to storytelling (i.e., its novelistic format) or its philosophical content that made it popular, however. Clearly, the reading public was most fascinated and delighted by the author's refined, elegant use of words and phrases. A noted critic of the time praised the "great good grace and sweet vogue [style] which eloquence has attained in our speech." The English language had progressed, he said,

because it has had the help of such rare and singular wits . . . among whom I think there is none [more important than] Master John Lyly . . . as he has stepped one step further therein than any other before or since he first began the witty discourse of his *Euphues,* whose works [feature] . . . apt words and sentences . . . fit phrases, pithy sentences . . . [and] flowing speech.[16]

pleasure-loving young man from Athens, which Elizabethan readers recognized as a thinly veiled version of Oxford. Euphues travels to Naples, which stands for London, and there meets the lovely Lucilla, fiancée of his friend, Philautus. In trying to woo her, Euphues alienates Philautus. But then the young woman runs off with a third man and the two friends are reunited. Woven into this thin plot are numerous long dissertations (lectures) on various social and philosophical subjects. In one of these sections, subtitled "On the Education of Youth," Lyly attacks the university in Athens (i.e., Oxford), depicting it as inadequate to the task of meeting the needs of its students.

The new prose style Lyly had invented subsequently became known as "Euphuism," after the chief character in the story. Though popular enough to warrant Lyly's writing a sequel—*Euphues and His England*—in 1580, later generations came to view Euphuism as an overly elaborate and artificial use of words. The style consists of repeated phrases utilizing such devices as alliteration (strings of words beginning with the same consonant, e.g., "the sad and silly seamstress"); antithesis (creating contrast between two ideas by balancing them side by side, e.g., "many are called, but few are chosen"); and rhyme.

A line from one of Lucilla's speeches in the first *Euphues* book illustrates Lyly's use of such devices: "In the coldest flint there is hot fire; the bee that has honey in her mouth has a sting in her tail; the tree that bears the sweetest fruit has a sour sap."[17] Here, "flint" and "fire," and later "sweetest" and "sour sap," are examples of alliteration; while the images of "coldest" and "hot," followed by "in her mouth" and "in her tail," and finally "sweetest" and "sour" balance one another as examples of antithesis. But though they create beautiful phrases, Lyly uses these devices in the book so often that they become, by modern standards, forced, highly repetitive, and overdone. Lyly's Euphuism, scholar Joseph Houppert points out, "is one of the few cases in literary history in which quantity determines quality."[18]

Moreover, the showiness and pomposity of Lyly's style was compounded by his relentless references to ancient and mythological characters, many of them very obscure. These are "so excessive and overwhelming," writes noted scholar John D. Wilson, "that it is difficult to see how even the idlest lady of Elizabeth's court found time or patience to wade through them."[19]

Lyly's First Plays

Yet many courtiers *did* wade through Lyly's novels. And this gave him mounting hope that he might produce more works, including plays, that would become popular in the royal court. The gritty, workaday grind of the professional theater interested him much less than the refined, elegant world of Elizabeth's court. More than anything else, Lyly dreamed of becoming a part of that world as her master of revels, the administrator in charge of dramatic and musical presentations for the queen and her nobles.

Lyly took the first steps designed to achieve his goal in 1580, shortly after the publication of the second *Euphues* book. He realized that gaining favor at court was dependent in large degree on knowing and exploiting the favors of high-placed people. So he took a job as secretary to Edward de Vere, the earl of Oxford and son-in-law of Lord Burleigh. Perhaps at the suggestion of de Vere, who was himself an amateur playwright, Lyly wrote two comic plays—*Campaspe* and *Sapho and Phao*—in 1583. The following year they were published and, thanks to de Vere's influence, also performed at court by two all-boys' troupes, the Children of the Royal Chapel and the Boys of St. Paul's Choir.

To the Elizabethans, who were used to comedies filled with foul language and having little in the way of structure and elegant phrases, Lyly's plays were a revelation. He eliminated profanity and other

This relief sculpture shows Queen Elizabeth and some of her courtiers, many of whom were well-read and familiar with the latest novels, poems, and plays.

base humor and substituted well-worded, witty passages that offered advice on romance and good manners and mocked those who pursued neither. Interspersed within each storyline were passages in which the actors sang and danced, always in a refined manner. Also, the plots were usually drawn from classical (Greek and Roman) history or mythology, giving them an air of intellectual sophistication. *Campaspe,* for example, tells the story of Greek conqueror Alexander the Great's love for a captive girl, Campaspe, and his eventual generosity and self-sacrifice in allowing her to rejoin the man she loves.

Here, too, Lyly displays a theme he would exploit in one way or another in most of his plays—namely, the idea that women were as intelligent and worthy as men. This was already becoming self-evident in a society ruled by a strong and cunning woman. Lyly's contribution was to emphasize the intrinsic worth of women by making them leading characters in drama. "The stage cannot be lighted by women's wit," Wilson explains,

> if the [members of the] audience have not yet realized that brain forms part of the feminine organism. In the days of Elizabeth, this realization began to dawn in men's minds; but it was Lyly who first expressed it in literature. . . . Those who preceded him were only dimly conscious of it, and therefore they failed to seize upon it as material for art. It was at court, the court of a

great virgin queen, that the equality of social privileges for women was first established; it was a courtier [i.e., Lyly] who introduced heroines into our drama.[20]

Qualities That Could Not Be Ignored

Lyly naturally saw the performance of his plays at court by the all-boys' companies as an opening to exploit in his quest for the position of master of revels. Taking the next logical step, in 1585 he took a part-time position as assistant master of

the St. Paul's Choir School. There, he wrote several plays for the young male scholars, staging them himself and perhaps sometimes even acting in them. *Gallathea* appeared between 1587 and 1588; *Endymion* in 1588; *Midas, Love's Metamorphosis,* and *Mother Bombie* around 1590; and *The Woman in the Moon* sometime between 1591 and 1595.

Of these, *Endymion,* subtitled *The Man in the Moon,* is now viewed as Lyly's masterpiece. He based it on the story of Endymion, a king in Greek mythology; the moon goddess loved him so much that she could not bear to see him die,

An eighteenth-century painting depicts Campaspe and Alexander the Great, the leading subjects in John Lyly's 1583 comic play, Campaspe.

so she put him into a deep, everlasting sleep. Lyly skillfully built on this simple framework, developing the story into a charming romance. In his version, Endymion rejects his former lover, the maiden Tellus, and makes advances on the moon goddess, Cynthia, who meets them coolly. Meanwhile, Tellus, seeking revenge, obtains the aid of a sorceress; the latter forces Endymion into a deep sleep from which, she claims, no one can awaken him. Cynthia hears what has happened and, taking pity on the young man, sends his best friend, Eumenides, to find a cure. He consults a magic fountain, which tells him that a kiss from Cynthia's lips will awaken Endymion. She gives that kiss and he wakes; but he suddenly realizes that he can never marry the goddess, whose powers and status are too lofty for the likes of a mere mortal. "None possessed my heart but Cynthia," he tells her, but "such a difference have the gods set between our states that all [that I feel for you] must be duty, loyalty, and reverence; nothing [that can] be termed love."[21]

This depiction of an ordinary man worshiping a superior woman was no accident. All who watched the play unfold realized that the character Cynthia represented Elizabeth, the virgin queen whom none of her male subjects dared to dream of wooing. In a similar vein, this and Lyly's other plays, written for performance at court as well as in the schools, are filled with indirect compliments to the queen.

In Lyly's Endymion, *the moon goddess Cynthia represented Queen Elizabeth, pictured here.*

Endymion and Lyly's other plays also feature the refined and elegant speech that was his trademark, although the flowery Euphuism so pervasive in his novels is significantly toned down in his dramatic works. One of Endymion's opening speeches, extolling Cynthia's virtues, illustrates how his alliteration and other literary devices are better integrated and less artificial sounding:

O fair Cynthia, why do others term you inconstant, whom I have never found unmovable? Injurious time, corrupt manners, unkind men, who, finding a constancy not to be matched in my sweet mistress, have christened her with the name of wavering, waxing, and waning! . . . There is nothing thought more admirable or commendable in the sea than the ebbing and flowing; and shall the moon, from whom the sea takes this virtue, be accounted fickle for increasing and decreasing?[22]

Modern readers unfamiliar with the works of other Elizabethan playwrights besides Shakespeare would likely assume that the preceding speech had been taken from one of his plays. And this is a tribute to Lyly's influence and importance in his age. Indeed, Wilson suggests, an attempt to trace Lyly's influence on later writers "would be to write a history of the Elizabethan stage."[23] Shakespeare and the others could not ignore his beautiful use of English prose, nor his liberal use of classical stories and themes, nor his dreamlike romantic settings and atmospheres. Shakespeare's *A Midsummer Night's Dream, Love's Labor's Lost, As You Like It,* and other romantic comedies

A ceiling panel for the Palazzo Fornese in Rome shows Cynthia about to kiss and awaken Endymion.

A still from the 1935 film version of A Midsummer Night's Dream, *a play influenced by Lyly.*

reverberate with prose writing, characters, and situations modeled on scenes from Lyly's plays.

Dreams Unfulfilled

Somehow during these busy years of writing *Endymion* and other plays, as well as producing them for private audiences, Lyly found the time to get married and have six children; to serve as a member of the British legislature, Parliament; and to help the bishop of London read and censor new books.

It was probably through his association with the bishop that Lyly became involved in the infamous "Marprelate" controversy. It was essentially a war of anonymous pamphlet writers that took place from the fall of 1588 to the summer of 1589. At least seven tracts appeared by someone who called himself Martin Marprelate, each attacking one or more well-known Episcopal bishops of the day or the Episcopal Church in general. It was clear to all who read the tracts that a Puritan had written them. At the time, the Puritans were a small, unpopular religious sect that the archbishop of Canterbury had been attempting to censor. To counter Marprelate's poisoned pen, several anti-Puritan pamphlets were issued in 1589; and scholars believe two of these—*Pappe with a Hatchet* and *A Whip for an Ape*—were composed by Lyly.

Unfortunately, none of these jobs—secretary to de Vere, assistant master at St. Paul's, censor and pamphlet writer for the bishop, and other odd endeavors—paid very much. Consequently, Lyly increasingly had trouble supporting his family and making ends meet. His dream of attaining the queen's well-paying, prestigious revels post always seemed to loom on the horizon; but for reasons uncertain, it always stayed out of reach.

Then, in 1591 came a new disappointment and personal setback for Lyly. The government shut down the all-boys' companies, and to make money, Lyly was forced to make his plays available for performance in the professional theater. Even this avenue earned him little, however, as playwrights did not make much income from the rights to their plays at that time. Exactly how Lyly earned a living in the 1590s is unclear. More certain is his extreme bitterness over his waning fortunes, especially his inability to gain the title of master of revels. In 1598, he wrote a sad and strongly worded letter to Elizabeth expressing his disappointment.

Evidently, the queen never answered Lyly, who after that sank still further into poverty and despair. Perhaps one last ray of sunshine for him followed her

King James I, who succeeded Elizabeth after her death, may have granted Lyly some land.

death in 1603. The following year, the bishop of Durham petitioned an official of the new ruler, King James, on Lyly's behalf. Recalling that the queen had made many promises to the playwright and broken them all, the bishop asked the government to act quickly because of Lyly's "years fast growing on [i.e., his increasing age] and his unsupportable charge of many children . . . besides the debt in which he stands."[24] The king may have indeed responded to this plea, for some evidence suggests that the crown granted Lyly a small grant of land in 1605.

If it happened, this gesture proved too little, too late. Lyly died the following year in obscure circumstances, still poor and bitter. If it is possible for poetic justice to make up for the unfulfilled dreams of such an individual after his passing, the courtly dreamer received his just rewards in the end. Regarding his contributions to the emerging English-speaking theater, "it is almost impossible to overestimate his historical importance," Wilson eloquently points out.

> This [is] not because he was a great genius or possessed of any magnificent artistic gifts, but for the simple reason that he happened to stand upon the threshold of modern English literature and at the very entrance to its splendid Elizabethan anteroom, and therefore all who came after felt something of his influence.[25]

Father of the Revenge Tragedy: Thomas Kyd

I f Lyly was the father of Elizabethan comic plays, Thomas Kyd deserves to be called one of the two fathers (along with Christopher Marlowe) of Elizabethan tragedy. Kyd's reputation rests almost solely on one play, although an extremely popular and influential one—*The Spanish Tragedy.* Indeed, in reviewing the surviving literature from the Elizabethan Age, scholars have found that this play was one of the three most frequently mentioned (along with Shakespeare's *Hamlet* and Marlowe's *Tamburlaine*). Moreover, Kyd's play created a new and widely popular literary genre—the "revenge tragedy." Numerous playwrights, including Shakespeare in his *Hamlet,* subsequently copied Kyd's format, and dozens of revenge tragedies

appeared on the English stage in the 1590s and early 1600s.

Yet rather surprisingly, despite Kyd's notable achievement, none of the surviving copies of *The Spanish Tragedy* bear his name. And for a long time, later scholars were not sure who wrote it. It was not until 1773 that a scholar named Thomas Hawkins unearthed a passing remark made by Elizabethan playwright Thomas Heywood in his 1612 essay, *Apology for Actors.* Heywood named Kyd as the undisputable author of the play. And later exhaustive scholarly studies of the text have verified this assertion.

The fact that in the century following Kyd's death people forgot about him and no longer connected his name with one of

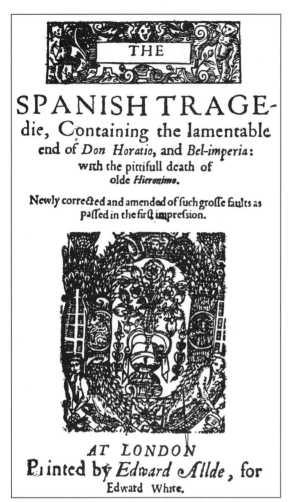

Thomas Kyd's name is conspicuously missing from this original title page of his play The Spanish Tragedy.

the most important English plays is, in and of itself, a tragedy. In that respect, it follows a pattern that began during the playwright's own lifetime. Indeed, tragedy in one form or another seemed to follow Kyd. On the one hand, he was fascinated by ancient Roman tragedy, and he wrote the first great tragedy of his era. On the

other, his sad final years and untimely death at age thirty-six constitute a tragedy in their own right, one that robbed the world of a unique talent.

Kyd's School Days

Relatively little is known about Kyd's early life. The records of the Church of St. Mary Woolnoth, in London, show that he was baptized there on November 6, 1558. So he was likely born a few days before. The same register names his father as Francis Kyd, a scrivener (a kind of scribe who copied letters and notarized documents). The family must have been of above-average means and social status; the elder Kyd was a prominent member of the local guild of scriveners (and eventually rose to become its director) and also an administrative helper at St. Mary's. In addition, the Kyds lived on Lombard Street, in one of the better sections of London. Two of their neighbors were prosperous publishers, one of whom, Thomas Hacket, would later end up printing some of Thomas Kyd's literary translations. Young Thomas's mother's name is disputed, but was probably either Anna or Agnes. Besides Thomas, she gave birth to two other children, a boy and a girl.

The only other firmly documented fact about Kyd's early years is his entry into the nearby respectable Merchant Taylors' School in November 1565 at the age of seven. Based on the knowledge he displayed in his later writing, Kyd must have learned a great deal in his school days. Like all young students of that era, he studied Latin and read from the works of the ancient Roman authors; that he was impressed by them is evident from his later literary references to the works of the playwright Seneca, orator Cicero, and poets Virgil, Tibullus, Propertius, Statius, Lucan, and Ovid. Kyd also learned a fair amount of French and Italian, which he would use later as a translator. He was far less conversant in history and geography, however, as his later writing contains frequent inaccuracies in these areas.

It is unknown exactly when Kyd left the Merchant Taylors' School. But one of his schoolmates, playwright Thomas Lodge, who was about the same age, left around 1573; so it is reasonable to assume that Kyd also departed around this time. Unlike Lodge, Marlowe, Greene, and most of the other university wits, Kyd apparently did not attend college. (Nevertheless, scholars still include him in their number because to a great degree he shared their background and training.) Instead, like Shakespeare, following grammar school Kyd was largely self-taught and learned by reading the classics and other literature.

Entry into the Theater

Reading was but a part-time endeavor for young Thomas Kyd, however, since he had to earn a living. His early jobs are uncertain. But considering that members of professional guilds usually expected their sons to follow in their footsteps, it is likely that he became an apprentice scrivener in his father's shop. The younger Kyd may also have been a teacher for a time.

Like so many aspects of Kyd's life, his inspiration for trying his hand in the theater is now a blank. Perhaps it was his deep love of ancient plays, especially those of the Roman master, Seneca. Whatever the reason, by the early 1580s he was working in some capacity with the Queen's Players, one of the more successful London theatrical companies. Part of the proof is a remark made in a pamphlet by dramatist Thomas Dekker: "In another company sat learned Watson, industrious Kyd, ingenious Achelly, and . . . inimitable Bentley."[26] Thomas Watson and Thomas Achelly were playwrights, and John Bentley was one of the leading Elizabethan actors; Bentley died in 1585, so Kyd must have been firmly established in the theater before that time.

A New Approach to Tragedy

Roughly two years after the death of his friend, Bentley, Kyd wrote *The Spanish Tragedy*. "It is one of those rare works," says noted scholar Philip Edwards, "in which a minor writer, in a strange inspiration, shapes the future by producing something quite new."[27] Indeed, Kyd's masterpiece represented a virtual quantum leap over what had come before in the tragic genre.

English writers had turned out tragedies before, especially during a period of unusual popularity in the 1560s. And many of these writers, like Kyd, had felt the influence of Seneca. The structure of Seneca's plays is very formal, and he drew his stories and characters from classical mythology and legend. Also, his plays are extremely serious in tone, emphasizing throughout such grave and weighty themes as murder, vengeance, and betrayal. It is significant that Seneca's works were not written specifically for performance on the stage; instead, they were recited in small, private gatherings. For this and other reasons, they were stately pieces lacking any real visual action; all murders and other mayhem were described in the past tense in long speeches by messengers or the narrator.

Some early English playwrights attempted to imitate Seneca's style. Their works, like his, were stately, slow-moving, talky, kept most violence offstage, and excluded comic characters and interludes. They were also presented in academic (school or court) settings, not in the public productions in town squares and inn yards; so they reached only limited audiences composed mostly of well-educated, well-read people. By contrast, strolling players enacted some plays involving murders and revenge for the public. These were more realistic and fast-paced than the academic tragedies but lacked good structure and retained periodic comic episodes to relieve the gloom.

Kyd's new approach was to combine the academic and popular traditions on the public stage and to improve on both of them in the process. "From Seneca," Thomas Parrott explains,

A drawing of the ancient Roman playwright Seneca, who influenced Kyd's work.

[he] drew a sense of structure, a division of the play into acts and scenes, no mere dramatized narrative, but a plot carefully built up with beginning, middle, and end, motivation, suspense, counter-action, and catastrophe. Kyd borrowed also some characteristic bits of Senecan tech-

nique—the revengeful ghost who opens the play, [and] the chorus. . . . From Seneca, too, Kyd gets his sense of style. He sternly excises [deletes] the old popular horse-play and buffoonery; what humor remains is grim and quite in keeping with the action. . . . From popular practice, on the other hand, Kyd drew his sense of the need for action on the stage; the most important events of his play are not reported, but represented before the eyes of the audience.[28]

In particular, most of the killing, of which there is a great deal in the play, takes place onstage, leaving the platform littered with bodies at the end. G.B. Harrison quips: "From Seneca, Kyd had drawn the notion that tragedy was to be measured by the number of the corpses."[29]

Bloody Revenge for Injustice

The result of this novel fusion of the classic and native dramatic styles was a well-constructed, gripping tale of murder and revenge that electrified audiences. A new theatrical genre—the "revenge play"—was born. A typical revenge play portrayed a hero seeking bloody justice for the wrongful acts of one or more "villains" and followed a specific formula, as described here by noted Shakespearean scholar Norrie Epstein:

Most of the play consists of the hero's plot to avenge an injustice or a crime committed against a family member. In their obsession with family honor and the violent means they'll take to preserve it, the characters of a revenge play resemble the tightly knit Corleone family in *The Godfather.* A rape, a dismemberment, or an act of incest might add sensationalism, and often a ghost incites the avenger to do his bloody business. By the last act, the stage is usually littered with carnage—much to everyone's delight.[30]

Other typical elements of revenge plays included the leading male character disguising himself or feigning insanity as part of his scheme to achieve vengeance, and the leading female character going mad and dying of grief.

The prototype of the style, *The Spanish Tragedy,* opens with the appearance of the two ghastly characters—the ghost of a slain Spanish courtier and Revenge. After they set the scene and foreshadow the tragic events to come, a meeting takes place at the Spanish court. Horatio, son of Hieronimo, chief marshal to the Spanish king, loves and expects to marry Belimperia, daughter of a Spanish duke. But Belimperia's brother, the evil, scheming Lorenzo, wants the young woman to wed Balthazar, a Portuguese prince. Lorenzo and Balthazar stab Horatio to death and leave him hanging from a garden arbor. On hearing of his son's brutal murder, Hieronimo becomes mad with grief. At first he is

The principal members of the Corleone family in the film The Godfather *resemble the leading characters in many Elizabethan revenge tragedies.*

unable to determine who has committed the crime, but he eventually discovers that Lorenzo and Balthazar are the culprits. Hieronimo decides to achieve his revenge by staging a play before the king and some visiting guests, including the fathers of Lorenzo and Balthazar. Hieronimo, Belimperia, Lorenzo, and Balthazar all take parts in the presentation. During the performance, Hieronimo stabs Lorenzo for real, but the audience assumes it is just part of the plot. Also, Belimperia kills Balthazar. Only when the

play is over do the spectators realize what has happened. Belimperia commits suicide, then Hieronimo does the same after slaying Lorenzo's father.

The influence of this story is immediately apparent in Shakespeare's *Hamlet,* in which the ghost of the title character's father asks him to get revenge for his murder and Hamlet traps the guilty party, his own uncle, by staging a play before the royal court. Also in *Hamlet,* as in Kyd's play, numerous other characters are drawn into the action and end up dead. And Shakespeare was only one of many Elizabethan playwrights who sought to emulate *The Spanish Tragedy*. The story of John Marston's *Antonio's Revenge* (1602), for example, tells how the ghost of the title character's father entreats the son to avenge his murder. Antonio does so through the device of a play staged at court, just as in *The Spanish Tragedy* and *Hamlet*. A similar situation occurs in George Chapman's *Revenge of Bussy d'Ambois* (ca. 1610). Bussy's ghost, who had reached that unwanted state through foul murder, asks his brother, Clermont, to achieve revenge for the crime. Other prominent examples of Elizabethan revenge tragedy inspired by Kyd's *Spanish Tragedy* include Shakespeare's *Titus Andronicus* (1593), Henry Chettle's *Tragedy of Hoffman* (1602), and Thomas Middleton's popular *Revenger's Tragedy* (1607).

The Question of the *Ur-Hamlet*

Kyd's influence on Shakespeare's *Hamlet* may well have been more fundamental than some similarities with the theme and plot of *The Spanish Tragedy*. Scholars have long agreed that one of the sources for the story told in *Hamlet*

Hamlet (standing at left) presents a play about a murder at the court of his royal uncle (seated at right), hoping to upset and trap him.

was the *Historia Danica,* a twelfth-century Latin work by Danish historian Saxo Grammaticus. A fair number of scholars are convinced that Shakespeare was even more influenced by another work based on the old Danish tale, a play that considerable evidence suggests may have been written by Thomas Kyd, performed often in the 1580s and 1590s, but subsequently lost. This play has come to be called the *Ur-Hamlet.* (The prefix "Ur" is a reference to the ancient Mesopotamian city of Ur, one of the first known human cities; its use in this manner usually denotes an "earlier" or "ancestral" version of something.)

Because the work in question no longer exists, no one can say for sure exactly what and how much it influenced Shakespeare and his associates. But it is tantalizing to speculate. To begin with, scholars widely agree that numerous words, lines, and constructions in Kyd's *Spanish Tragedy* are strikingly similar to words, lines, and constructions in Shakespeare's *Hamlet,* especially in the version known as the First Quarto. (A majority of scholars accept that this mutilated rendition of *Hamlet* was pieced together by actors after the fact, partly from their memories of Shakespeare's original and partly from additions they threw in from older plays, including *The Spanish Tragedy* and the *Ur-Hamlet.*) Take, for instance, this line from the First Quarto, spoken by Hamlet's mother, Queen Gertrude:

I will conceal, consent, and do my best, whatever strategy you shall devise.[31]

Compare it with the following exchange between Belimperia and Hieronimo:

Belimperia: Hieronimo, I will consent, conceal, and aught that may effect for your avail. . . .

Hieronimo: On then; whatsoever I devise, let me entreat you, grace my practices.[32]

There is little doubt that these and other textual elements in various versions of *Hamlet* were borrowed from Kyd's *Spanish Tragedy.* And it is not a great leap to suggest that other elements of Shakespeare's great play might have been borrowed from the lost *Ur-Hamlet* so often credited to Kyd. The late Frederick Boas, a leading scholar of Elizabethan drama, provides the following plausible reconstruction of the possible series of events leading from Kyd's conjectured *Ur-Hamlet* to Shakespeare's more famous version:

The *Ur-Hamlet* was written by Kyd, probably in the latter part of 1587, and resembled *The Spanish Tragedy* in style and technique. It did not, however, become as popular as its sister play. . . . [The *Ur-Hamlet* was performed on Elizabethan stages off and on] for fifteen years before Shakespeare began to handle it. During this period, it probably underwent, in manuscript form, a certain amount of adaptation to suit the rapid changes of popular taste, or the circumstances of different [acting] companies. Thus, when Shakespeare . . . began in 1602 [or slightly earlier] to remodel the *Ur-Hamlet,* he [likely based it] not on Kyd's play in its primitive form, but a popularized stage version of it. Shakespeare himself, in his first revision, kept in the last three acts considerable portions of this version. Evidences of Kyd's hand . . . [are] scattered sufficiently through the text to vindicate his share in the creation of the modern world's most wonderful tragedy. . . . *Hamlet* in its final form . . . [is a fusion] of the inventive dramatic craftsmanship of Thomas Kyd, and the majestic imagination, penetrating psychology, and rich verbal music of William Shakespeare.[33]

Kyd's Final Tragedy

The events of Kyd's life immediately following the appearance of *The Spanish Tragedy* are uncertain. He may have written other plays, either on his own or in collaboration with other writers; but if so, the works are either lost or cannot be firmly connected to him. A remark in a letter by playwright Thomas Nashe asserts that Kyd gave up writing plays in 1588 to become a translator of Italian. And other evidence suggests that in the late 1580s Kyd went to

work for a wealthy nobleman, perhaps as a tutor. The identity of this employer is unknown; possible candidates include Robert Radcliffe; Lord Fitzwalter; Henry Herbert, earl of Pembroke; and Lord Strange, patron of a company of players, Lord Strange's Men. More certain is that about 1591, Kyd shared lodgings with fellow playwright Christopher Marlowe.

As it turned out, Kyd's connection with Marlowe contributed indirectly to the former's untimely and tragic end. In May 1593, government authorities arrested Kyd on suspicion that he had taken part in some recent attacks on London's

A document belonging to Kyd's roommate, Christopher Marlowe (pictured here), got Kyd into trouble with the government.

foreign craftsmen (a charge that was almost certainly false). Making matters worse, a search of Kyd's rooms revealed a manuscript containing atheistic statements, which the government frowned on at the time. He claimed the essay belonged to Marlowe and had somehow gotten into his own papers when they had roomed together. After undergoing severe torture, Kyd was released; but his employer was not convinced of his innocence and dismissed him.

Desperate, the playwright wrote to a high government official, Sir John Puckering, begging him to use his influence to help get his job back, but to no avail. Disgraced and poverty-stricken, Kyd died in obscurity the following year. A few months later, his parents refused to administer his estate, probably to escape having to pay his considerable debts. Over the course of the next few generations, people forgot that Kyd had written *The Spanish Tragedy*. And by the mid–eighteenth century, he himself had been forgotten. Fortunately, the diligent efforts of scholars eventually revealed his contributions to English drama and illuminated his twin tragedies—the one he had written and the one he had lived.

Poet of Pageant and Drama: George Peele

George Peele's main claim to fame may well be that he was one of the most energetic of the Elizabethan university wits and perhaps the most versatile (though Christopher Marlowe was certainly more skilled). Whatever their talents, most of the others stuck largely to one style or genre. John Lyly and Robert Greene wrote mostly romantic comedies, for instance, and Thomas Kyd concentrated on tragedy. By contrast, Peele tried his hand in a wide variety of genres, including history, pastoral romance, tragedy, and civic pageant.

Two things Peele had in common with most of his fellow university wits were his short life and appallingly brief literary career. He died at the age of thirty-six,

while Thomas Nashe was dead at thirty-four, Kyd at thirty-six, Greene at thirty-two, and Marlowe at twenty-nine. Peele's career as a professional dramatist lasted only about ten years or so. He had barely begun to express his literary powers when death cut him short, and an examination of his surviving plays shows a marked improvement in quality over time. Had he lived another twenty years and continued writing plays, he might have become one of the greatest of English dramatists.

What Peele did manage to do in his short stint in the theater was to help in the ongoing and rapid transformation of English native drama, especially for consumption by public audiences. On the one hand, he familiarized these audiences with mythological characters and stories that had long been the subjects mainly of private theatrical productions in the schools and the royal court. Peele also captured the homely, picturesque aspects of English country life without making its characters sound base and illiterate. In fact, he was an excellent poet who, along with Lyly and Marlowe, did much to improve the language of the dramas presented in the theaters and other public venues. Thus, Peele is best seen as one of a group of pioneers who paved the way for greater artists such as Shakespeare and Jonson. One of Peele's modern biographers writes:

> Out of this glorious period, the Golden Age of English literature, emerges . . . a writer whose life was as intense, colorful, and turbulent as the era itself. The Elizabethan Age was one of daring discoveries, intrepid explorers, and bold pioneers. George Peele was of that age, that age of pioneers. His life was short and crowded; he traced with a brilliant and fitful light a brief trail across the sky, a portent of much greater things to come.[34]

James Peele and the Civic Pageants

George Peele was probably born in the parish of St. James Garlickhithe, in London, not far southeast of the famous St. Paul's Cathedral. The register of St. James preserves the record of a baptism of a child named George Peele on July 25, 1556; and though the chance exists that he was not the dramatist, most modern scholars accept that he was.

George Peele was born near London's famous St. Paul's Cathedral.

His father, James Peele, was a Londoner who served as chief administrator for Christ's Hospital, which adjoined Christ's Church, an important Elizabethan landmark. The elder Peele kept the hospital's records and did his best to look after his family, which included his first wife, Anne, and at least five other children besides George. The family dwelled in modest quarters nestled on the church grounds.

In his spare time, James Peele also dabbled in writing a popular form of entertainment of his era—the civic pageant. He must have passed on his enthusiasm for these presentations to his son, for the younger Peele later composed some of the finest examples of the genre. The civic pageants were not formal plays with structured plots, character development, and so on. They were instead brief outdoor displays of pomp and ceremony intended to celebrate important civic events, especially the inauguration of the lord mayor of London. The new mayor, along with other dignitaries, town officials, soldiers, musicians, and various colorfully costumed entertainers, took part in a gala parade through the city's streets. Scholar Leonard Ashley describes one that took place in 1553:

> Two tall men led the way, bearing great streamers emblazoned with [the coat of] arms [of the new mayor's family]. Then came [men dressed] in blue silk playing a drum, a flute, and a fife, followed by two woodmen in green . . . wearing shields on their backs, carrying clubs and burning fireworks. . . . These woodmen . . . were standard for all pageants. After the woodmen marched sixteen trumpeters blowing lustily, then seventy men in blue gowns, caps and hose, each with a shield and javelin. [Then came the musicians], the lord mayor's officers, the lord mayor himself, with two henchmen [bodyguards], and finally the aldermen and sheriffs.[35]

At some point, the procession stopped for a short while and watched a pageant presented atop a wooden platform erected on a wagon. Some of the entertainers posed or performed mimes, while others presented speeches congratulating and flattering the new mayor and singing the praises of London and England. James Peele became adept at writing these speeches, as George Peele did later.

Education and Career Path

It is not likely, however, that as a boy George Peele actually aspired to write either pageants or plays for a living. Neither of these were considered legitimate literature at the time, nor did they pay very well. The career path that he and his father mapped out for him is unknown, but a brief review of the young man's education offers some clues. The primary schools George Peele attended were all in the Christ's Church complex. From age nine to fourteen, he studied in the "upper school" under a stern headmaster, Ralph Waddington, who emphasized religious instruction as well as Latin and Greek.

Waddington's goal was to prepare his male students for higher studies at Oxford. And he succeeded in the case of Peele, who left London for Oxford in March 1571. That university consisted of a number of smaller colleges, each of which specialized in one or two areas of study. Peele eventually entered Christ Church College, the largest of the Oxford subdivisions. The stress there on theology and moral philosophy was strong, and a good many of the graduates went on to become clergymen; so it is entirely possible that he started out with that goal.

Yet Peele did not go on to a life in the Church, and in fact ended up in the theater, a profession that most churchmen viewed as cheap and disreputable. This might be attributable to two factors. First, like so many other young men at Oxford, Peele had some involvement with play presentation. One of his kinsmen, William Gager, who wrote plays in Latin for private productions, later recalled that Peele translated one of the works of the ancient Greek playwright Euripides. Then, after graduation, Peele returned to Oxford to help Gager stage some plays in honor of the visit of a Polish nobleman; Peele apparently supervised the costumes, scenery, and fireworks and other special effects. It may be, therefore, that the young man eventually decided on a career

in the theater because he had come to love putting on plays.

The other factor that may have contributed to Peele's choice of the theater over the clergy was his propensity for "having a good time." When he reached Oxford, he found himself drawn into the ranks of the more undisciplined element common to college life in all ages—in this case those pleasure-seeking young men who spent more time partying and cavorting at local taverns than studying. Somehow, he did manage to complete his courses and graduate; but the fast-living, somewhat scandalous atmosphere of the London theater scene may have appeared increasingly attractive to him.

This does not mean that Peele was a ne'er-do-well who did not take the idea

A contemporary drawing depicts Christ Church College at Oxford, one of the schools Peele attended.

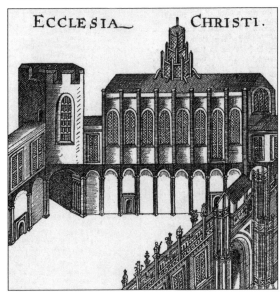

50

of earning a living seriously; in fact, all available evidence suggests that he, like Lyly, Greene, Nashe, and many other young playwrights of that era, was a hard worker who struggled to support himself and his family. (He married a sixteen-year-old girl, Anne Cooke, in 1580, and they subsequently had at least two daughters.) Though over time Peele gained a particularly bad reputation as a playboy and lowlife character, most modern scholars remain unconvinced. "There is no proof whatever," says Ashley, "that Peele was any more sensual or violent than his age, any more unrestrained than the average Elizabethan or more bohemian than the average writer."[36]

In this drawing depicting "The Judgment of Paris," the three goddesses demand that Paris choose which of them is the fairest.

Flattery for the Queen

In fact, Peele wasted little time in attempting to make a living in the London theater. Sometime in the early 1580s he wrote *The Arraignment of Paris,* which was performed at the royal court in front of the queen. It is the earliest surviving example of a pastoral play—that is, one that takes place in a rural setting and idealizes the pleasures of country life. It is also the first play about ancient mythology in English (rather than Latin), a bold attempt to bring lofty literary themes to the popular stage.

The play's story is based loosely on the famous myth usually called "The

Judgment of Paris." Paris, a prince of the ancient city of Troy, is tending his flocks on the pastoral slopes of Mt. Ida, when he is called on to choose which of three goddesses—Juno, Minerva, or Venus—is the fairest. He chooses Venus, which angers the other two. In Peele's version, Juno and Minerva arraign Paris (take him to court, here one presided over by the gods), accusing him of bias, and the court eventually defers the case to another goddess, Diana. She prudently refrains from judging among the three divine contestants, awarding the prize instead to a minor goddess, Eliza, who rules a distant, admirable kingdom.

"She gives laws of justice and of peace," Diana declares,

> And on her head, as fits her fortune best, she wears a wreath of laurel, gold, and palm; her robes of purple and scarlet dye; her veil of white, as best befits a maid. . . . This peerless nymph [nature goddess], whom heaven and earth love . . . this is she in whom do meet so many gifts in one, on whom our country gods so often gaze.[37]

Eliza and her kingdom are clearly not in the original myth, but rather additions representing Queen Elizabeth and her England. Like so many other London playwrights, Peele hoped to advance himself by flattering the queen.

A Diverse Theatrical Corpus

If this device was an attempt to gain Peele a position as a court dramatist, it failed. No other invitations to perform at court materialized, and he thereafter concentrated on turning out material for the public stages. Another play based on mythology, *The Hunting of Cupid,* soon followed; unfortunately only a few fragments of it survive. Then came several plays that have survived complete: *The Battle of Alcazar* (ca. 1588), *The Old Wives' Tale* (ca. 1589), *Edward I* (ca. 1590–1593), and *The Love of King David and Fair Bethsabe* (published in 1599 but written at an unknown earlier date).

One is immediately struck by the wide variety of themes and genres of these works. *Paris* and *Cupid* were lightweight pastoral romances; *Alcazar* a tragedy about swashbucklers in wartime; *Wives' Tale* a comic fairy tale; *Edward* a historical drama; and *David and Bethsabe* a biblical drama, in fact the only Elizabethan play based solely on the Bible. In writing these plays, Peele showed a creative versatility and flexibility matched by few other playwrights of the period.

Performances of the works in this diverse theatrical corpus also infused the public theaters with poetic verses of unusual quality and beauty. (Up until the late 1580s, only Lyly's verses were comparable; but his were aimed mainly at courtly audiences rather than public ones.) Peele's dramatic poetry reached its height of beauty and effectiveness in *David and Bethsabe,* which one nineteenth-century English critic called "the earliest fountain of pathos and harmony that can be traced in our dramatic poetry."[38] Both actors and audiences must have delighted in the following nimble, dreamy words of love spoken by David in the opening scene:

> Now comes my lover tripping like the roe [small deer],
>
> And brings my longings tangled in her hair.
>
> To joy her love I'll build a kingly bower [garden house made of vines]
>
> Seating in hearing [earshot] of a hundred streams. . . .

One of many Renaissance paintings of David and Bathsheba (or Bethsabe). In the biblical tale, David, king of Israel, covets Bethsabe even though she is married to another.

Open the doors and entertain my love,

Open I say and as you open, sing

"Welcome fair Bethsabe, King David's darling."[39]

Commemorative Poems and Pageants

Peele also utilized his abilities as a poet to make extra money outside the profes-sional theater. Among the poems he composed for ceremonial and commem-orative occasions were *A Congratulatory Eclogue, The Honor of the Garter,* and *The Praise of Chastity.* In at least one case, such verses were motivated as much by Peele's deep sense of patriotism as by the need for cash. In 1588, Spain launched its mighty Armada, which the English forces defeated. In retaliation, in April 1589 Elizabeth sent the so-called counter-Armada, a fleet of some 150 ships, to capture the rich Azores island group and overthrow the Spanish king. To commemorate the launch, Peele penned the seventy-six-line *A Farewell to Norris and Drake,* honoring the expedition's two leaders in the title. In a note accompanying the poem, Peele wrote:

> Your virtues famed by your fortunes, and fortunes renowned by your virtues . . . together with the admiration the world has worthily conceived of your worthiness, have at this time encouraged me . . . to send my short farewell to our English forces. . . . [I dedicate this poem to them] beseeching God mercifully and miraculously . . . to defend fair England, that her soldiers may in their departure be fortunate, and in their return triumphant.[40]

Though written in prose, the letter displays the obvious hand of a poet in its frequent examples of alliteration: famed/fortunes, world/worthily, farewell/forces, and mercifully/miraculously.

Still another way Peele applied his poetic talents was in writing speeches for the same London lord mayor's pageants his father had. For the inauguration of Sir Wolstan Dixi, on October 29, 1585, George Peele supplied *The Device of the Pageant Borne Before Wolstan Dixi, Lord Mayor of the City of London.* The opening speech of the work—the earliest surviving complete text of a lord mayor's pageant—

Sir Francis Drake, whom Peele honored in A Farewell to Norris and Drake.

begins with a song of praise for the city itself. Here, Peele's sense of patriotism shines through: "Lo lovely London rich and fortunate, famed through the World for peace and happiness, is here advanced and set in Highest seat."[41] The speaker goes on to thank God and to praise Queen Elizabeth. Then several children, assuming the roles of London, the Thames, Loyalty, the Soldier, the Sailor, Science, and others, give speeches. (In an actual performance, they stood on the pageant wagon, a sort of float, accompanied by costumed clowns, devils, and other characters, as well as fireworks displays.)

A Rapid and Fatal Decline

It is unknown what Peele earned each year from his dramatic and poetic endeavors. Whatever it was, it evidently was not enough to make ends meet, for he fell increasingly into debt in the early 1590s. Making matters worse, he seems to have endured some kind of chronic illness that sapped his strength. On January 17, 1595, he wrote a letter begging for aid from Lord Burleigh, the same nobleman whom Lyly had asked for help in getting a position at Oxford. The letter, which the playwright's daughter hand-delivered, has survived and reads in part:

> Pardon great patron of learning and Virtue this rude encounter, in that I presume, a scholar of so mean merit [limited accomplishments], to present your wisdom with this small manual [manuscript], by this simple messenger, my eldest daughter. . . . Long sickness having so enfeebled me makes [my] bashfulness almost become impudency [insolence].[42]

The manuscript Peele's daughter carried along with the letter was *The Tale of Troy,* a poem the writer had penned as a young man. He hoped that Burleigh would buy it, affording him some ready cash. But for his own reasons, the lord ignored the plea.

After this rebuke, Peele's decline was rapid and fatal. A London church register recorded his death less than two years later—on November 9, 1596. Contemporary literary critic Francis Meres supplied an epitaph, asserting that the playwright had died "by the pox."[43] This was an unkind jab, since at the time "the pox" meant syphilis, a serious sexually transmitted disease, which implied that Peele had associated with prostitutes and other "bad" people. Whether this was indeed the "long sickness" mentioned in the letter to Burleigh will probably never be known. What is certain is that Meres's remark bolstered in the minds of later critics the idea that Peele himself was a bad person, as one writer put it, "a product of London streets and gutters."[44]

Fortunately for Peele, the passage of several centuries and some serious evaluation of his plays have been kinder to him; today, people judge him for his talents rather than for how he may have lived his life. And he is now rightfully seen as one of the innovative popular dramatists from whom the master— Shakespeare—learned his craft.

Chapter 5

A Man at War Within Himself: Robert Greene

Influential and controversial in his own time, Robert Greene was one of the more important and perhaps the most colorful of the Elizabethan playwrights. On the professional level, he penned the first widely successful romantic comedies for the public theaters; and these strongly influenced Shakespeare and others who later perfected this genre. On the private level, by contrast, Greene's influence was of a psychological and supportive nature, as he befriended some of the major dramatists of the London scene, including Thomas Lodge, Thomas Nashe, George Peele, and Christopher Marlowe.

What made Greene controversial, then and now, was that he was a man of extremes. He had perhaps the shortest professional career of any Elizabethan playwright, for example—a mere four years or less (roughly 1587 to 1591); yet his output of both plays and prose stories was large and noteworthy. Nashe, a frequent eyewitness to his friend's working habits, left behind this description of the remarkable speed at which Greene produced material, much of it well written:

In a night and day would he [turn out] a pamphlet as well as [someone else could have done] in seven years, and glad was the printer that might be so blessed to pay him dear for the very dregs of his wit.[45]

An even more dramatic contrast can be seen between the nature of Greene's private life and that of his writings. One of the first English autobiographers, he turned out numerous tracts describing his own life (usually through the actions of a fictional character); and these reveal a sordid existence characterized by excessive drinking, carousing, and association with prostitutes, thieves, and other ele-

This engraving from a 1597 pamphlet shows Robert Greene's friend, playwright Thomas Nashe.

ments of London's seamy underworld. Yet in theme and execution, his works are just the opposite. As the late, noted literary scholar William Neilson put it:

In spite of the self-confessed wickedness of his ways, Greene was not a hardened criminal, and no themes are more frequent in his tracts than moral exhortation and repentance. It is further notable that his work is freer from grossness than that of most of his contemporary playwrights, and he is distinguished for the freshness and purity of his female creations. He seems also, to judge from his plays, to have retained a love for the country, where he often chose to lay his scenes; and he ranks high among the lyricists [intense, exuberant, colorful writers] of the time.[46]

A Wild Youth

Greene came into the world in early July 1558 in Norwich (located about ninety miles northeast of London). His parents were middle class and respectable, in his own later words serious and honest people to whose "wholesome advice"[47] he regrettably turned a deaf ear. He probably attended the Norwich Free Grammar School. That institution awarded scholarships for Corpus Christi College, one of the subdivisions of nearby Cambridge University; and the register of Corpus Christi lists Greene as entering that school in the spring of 1573, when he was about fifteen. The young man received his B.A.

An etching captures the seamy atmosphere of a London saloon in the late 1700s. Prostitutes, thieves, and other disreputable characters also frequented such places in Greene's day.

from Cambridge about 1579 and later acquired an M.A. at Oxford. Clearly, his extensive education rendered him eminently qualified to join the ranks of the London literary group that became known as the university wits.

Apparently Greene received more than an education at Cambridge. He also found himself exposed to the same kind of rule breakers, heavy drinkers, and troublemakers Peele had encountered at Oxford. However, if Peele merely dabbled in youthful vice, Greene became a master of it, and by his own admission. In one of his last works, *Repentance,* he sadly recalled

that at Cambridge he fell in "amongst wags [young men] as lewd [indecent] as myself, with whom I consumed [used up] the flower of my youth."[48]

Greene and some of his cohorts eventually ran wild beyond the limits of Cambridge and even of England itself. During breaks from their classes, they traveled to Italy and Spain, where, he later admitted, "I saw and practiced such villainy as is abominable [horrible] to declare."[49] To get the money for these trips, Greene approached and lied to his father, who evidently thought his son was using the funds for respectable purposes.

Romantic Adventures, Fictional and Real

Increasingly, young Robert Greene became unhappy, aimless, restless, and unsure about the future. In his own words, he "seemed so discontent that no place would please me to abide in, nor no vocation cause me to stay myself in."[50] So after graduating from the university, he drifted to London, where he lived for a time by borrowing money from his former school friends. When they would no longer extend him credit, in desperation he turned to the only way he could conceive of using his considerable literary talents to make money. This is how Greene began writing stories and eventually plays for popular consumption.

Sometime between 1580 and 1583, the young man wrote the first of a long series of what he termed "Love Pamphlets" because they dealt in one way or another with the subject of love and romance. These were not pamphlets in the modern sense (i.e., short informational tracts), but long prose stories. *Mamillia, a Mirror or Looking Glass for the Ladies of England,* in two parts, is set in Padua, a colorful Italian location which Greene had likely visited. It tells the story of a young man, Pharicles, who falls in love with Mamillia, the daughter of the local ruler.

She returns his love. But then Pharicles meets and falls madly in love with another attractive young woman. The noble and forgiving Mamillia twice takes him back and even helps him escape from prison, where he had been confined after a relationship with a prostitute. Finally, Pharicles and Mamillia are married and achieve happiness.

As in many other stories he penned, Greene injected into *Mamillia* what were almost certainly strong autobiographical elements. The frivolous, morally confused young Pharicles certainly closely resembles the young Robert Greene; and it is

This 1598 woodcut is the only known surviving depiction of Robert Greene.

possible that one or more of the female characters are modeled on young women he met when he was in Italy. In any case, Mamillia is the first of Greene's strong, well-developed female characters, for, like Lyly, he was a pioneer in emphasizing the intrinsic worth of women. Lyly was the first to do it in plays, but in the same period Greene was blazing the trail in prose stories.

While turning out more prose romances, including *Pandosto* and *Menaphon*, Greene himself had a brush with *real* romance. Late in 1585 or early in 1586, he met and married a young woman named Dorothy, the daughter of a country gentleman. They had a son soon afterward. But Greene did not give up his drinking and carousing, and his irresponsible behavior rapidly ruined the marriage. "As much as she would [try to] persude me from my willful wickedness," he later wrote, "after I had a child by her I cast her off, having spent up [all] the marriage money [dowry] which I [had] obtained by her [i.e., from her father]. Then I left her."[51] Some evidence shows that at the time Greene left Dorothy, he was carrying on with the sister of one of London's most notorious gangsters, a man known as "Cutting Ball." The product of this affair was another son, this time born out of wedlock.

Greene's Plays

Among the other characters of questionable reputation with whom Greene mingled in London were playwrights, including Nashe, whom he had known since his Cambridge days. Perhaps influenced by them, about 1587 Greene decided to try his hand at drama. His first effort, *Alphonsus, King of Arogon* (first produced in 1588), was consciously modeled on Marlowe's *Tamburlaine the Great,* produced the year before. In each case, the hero rises through the ranks to lofty power and ends up marrying the daughter of his enemy. The difference is that Marlowe's work is well conceived and well executed, while Greene's is but a weak and pale imitation. The next two plays by Greene—*A Looking Glass for London and England* (ca. 1590), written with Thomas Lodge, and *Orlando Furioso* (ca. 1591)—were better than his first; but if these three plays had been his only theatrical works, his name would surely have become as obscure as those of the majority of the two-hundred-plus playwrights of the period.

Greene's deserved importance as an Elizabethan dramatist rests on his next two plays—*The Honorable History of Friar Bacon and Friar Bungay* (ca. 1591) and *The Scottish History of James IV, Slain at Flodden* (ca. 1591). The first was perhaps the most skillfully written English stage comedy up to that time. It contains two cleverly interwoven plots. The first is a romantic tale about the love of Edward, a former prince of Wales (and later King Edward I) for Margaret, a noble maiden. Edward is angry when he finds out that Margaret loves another man, Lord Lacy; but the prince eventually gives her up and blesses her union with Lacy.

The other story that unfolds in the play concerns the larger-than-life thirteenth-century Oxford scholar Roger Bacon, whom legend claimed was a powerful magician. In Greene's romance, Bacon, aided by Friar Bungay, constructs a human head made of brass, and with the help of the Devil they endow it with speech. Bacon hopes to learn from the head how he might encircle England with a huge brass wall, making it safe from foreign invaders. The problem is that no one knows when the head will begin talking. Bacon watches it day and night for three weeks, but it remains silent. So he has his servant, Miles, watch it while he goes to

Medieval Oxford scholar Roger Bacon, one of the title characters in Greene's most famous play.

sleep. The head then speaks two words—"Time is"—but Miles thinks this utterance too trivial to bother waking his master. The head speaks twice more, saying "Time was" and "Time is past," then a flash of lightning appears and the brass artifact falls to the floor and shatters. Waking, Bacon learns what has happened and explodes at Miles:

> Villain! Time is past! My life, my fame, my glory, all are past. Bacon, the turrets of your hope are ruined down. Your seven years [of] study lie in the dust! Your Brazen Head lies broken through [the negligence of] a slave that watched. . . . Villain, if you had called to Bacon then, if you had watched, and waked the sleepy friar . . . the Brazen Head [would] have uttered aphorisms [great truths] and England would be circled round with brass.[52]

Greene's other masterpiece, *James IV*, was the first full-length English tragicomedy in that it skillfully blended a serious plot about courtly love, intrigue, betrayal, and attempted murder with elements of humor and pure fantasy. The story of James, who is married to an English princess but loves a Scottish countess, is told as a sort of play within a play; in an imaginary setting, Oberon, king of the fairies, watches James's story performed by a group of fairy actors.

Most modern scholars accept that the style, tone, and characters of some of

Greene's plays later influenced a number of Shakespeare's works. According to the late J.M. Brown, for instance, *"Friar Bacon and Friar Bungay* (with Marlowe's *Faustus*) preceded Shakespeare's use of the supernatural; the fairy framework of *James IV* is followed by [Shakespeare's] *A Midsummer Night's Dream* [which also takes place in a fairy setting and features a fairy king named Oberon]."[53]

Greene's Attack on Shakespeare

In fact, Shakespeare's borrowings from Greene and other contemporary playwrights may have been the basis for the latter's open dislike for Shakespeare. It was not unusual in those days for one writer to take the plots, ideas, and characters of others and rework them in various ways in his own plays. There was (and remains) a rather fine line between artistic influence and out-and-out plagiarism; and Greene appears to have felt that Shakespeare had somehow crossed that line. One of Greene's principal modern biographers, the late Russian scholar Nicholas Storojenko, wrote:

Nearly every one of Shakespeare's juvenile [early] productions . . . [was based on an original] in the dramatic literature of the [mid-to-late 1580s]. So long as he was content with writing for his own company . . . Greene and his friends, who wrote for other companies . . .

[cared little]. But when . . . he began to widen his sphere of action and to offer his services to other companies, when he [threatened] to flood the theaters of London with his productions, then all Greene's clique were up in arms against him, with Greene himself at their head. . . . Greene saw in Shakespeare, not only a successful rival, but an enemy who beat the established dramatists with their own weapons, which he had stolen from them.[54]

Greene's indignation bubbled to the surface in a 1592 pamphlet titled *Groatsworth of Wit, Bought with a Million of Repentance.* The attack on Shakespeare reads in part:

Based-minded men [are] all three of you [Nashe, Peele, and Marlowe], if by my misery you be not warned. . . . For there is an upstart Crow, beautified with our feathers [made famous by stealing our material], that with his *Tiger's heart wrapped in a player's hide,* supposes that he is as well able to bombast out [i.e., write] a blank verse as [well as] the best of you; and being an absolute *Johannes fac totum* [jack of all trades, in this case an actor and playwright for different companies], is in his own conceit the only Shake-scene [a parody of Shakespeare's name] in the country. O that I might entreat [beg] your rare wits to be employed

Greene disliked William Shakespeare (pictured here) and attacked him for "stealing" material from others.

should be subject to the pleasures [whims] of such rude grooms [another jab at what he sees as thankless actors].[55]

(The charge that Shakespeare had a "Tiger's heart wrapped in a player's hide" is a parody of "O tiger's heart wrapped in a woman's hide," a line from act 1, scene 4 of Shakespeare's *Henry VI, Part 1,* produced in London earlier that same year.)

After considerable study of all the available evidence, modern scholars are convinced that Greene's inference that Shakespeare had plagiarized other dramatists was overblown. Shakespeare, Brown pointed out,

was doing just what other playwrights did, what Greene himself did. . . . Greene and the other university men dramatized from the old chroniclers—as Shakespeare often did too—and from Italian, Latin, and Greek authors. Shakespeare generally preferred to take what was readiest at hand.[56]

in more profitable courses [i.e., choose some other profession] and let those apes [actors who speak Shakespeare's lines] imitate your past excellence . . . for it is [a] pity [that] such rare wits [as you are],

It is more likely that Greene's attack was motivated out of a combination of jealousy for a rival who was clearly a better writer and Greene's bitterness over his own past mistakes.

A Moral Conversion

That bitterness was probably a by-product of the major moral conversion Greene had undergone in the months leading up to *Groatsworth of Wit.* The pamphlet was only one of a series of tracts he published describing the dangers and wastefulness of the kind of life he had lived for many years. Two others were *Farewell to Folly* (1591) and *Repentance,* penned on his deathbed in August 1592. Greene hoped these writings would steer other young men toward more positive and constructive behaviors than his own. He also attempted to do society a service by exposing many of the tricks and schemes used by London thieves and swindlers against unwary residents and visitors. The vehicle was another series of pamphlets, which appeared in late 1591 and early 1592, among them *A Notable Discovery of Cozenage, The Black Book's Messenger,* and *The Second Part of Cony-Catching.* (A cony was a "rabbit," or the gullible victim of a thief or conman; today such a victim would be called a "mark.") In response to this courageous campaign, some underworld figures threatened to cut off the playwright's hand and even tried to kill him.

The attempt on Greene's life failed. But within months he was dead anyway, largely because years of heavy drinking and other bad habits, compounded by overwork, had taken a terrible toll on his system. He became ill in early August 1592 after consuming too much wine and pickled herring at a party. Poverty-stricken and bedridden in a rented room owned by a shoemaker, the writer grew steadily weaker over the course of the month; and only his mistress (Cutting Ball's sister) and landlord and landlady took the time to comfort him in his final days. On September 2, he hastily scribbled a note to Dorothy, the wife he had abandoned a few years before. After begging her to pay his landlords the back rent he owed them, he implored, "Forget and forgive my wrongs done to you, and Almighty God have mercy on my soul. Farewell till we meet in heaven, for on earth you will never see me more."[57]

Robert Greene died the following day. The thoughtful manner of his departure, along with his recent efforts to make amends for his past mistakes, stood in stark contrast to the callous way he had earlier treated both himself and others. But this was fitting, for he was ever a man at war within himself. Indeed, he had long been host to a relentless battle between his baser impulses and the moral ideals expressed in his writings. In the end, to his credit, his good side won.

Risk Taker and Mystery Maker: Christopher Marlowe

odern scholars agree that Chris-topher Marlowe was the most accomplished and important English play-wright before Shakespeare. This opinion is based on Marlowe's several literary contributions to the emerging art of dra-matic writing. First and foremost was his talent as a poet and his placement of refined, polished, and moving verses in the mouths of his characters. Some of his contemporaries, notably Lyly and Peele, had proven themselves capable poets and had improved the quality of the English spoken by actors. But Marlowe was more than merely capable; he was the first truly great poet to write plays in English. More specifically, Marlowe recognized the po-tential power and beauty of blank verse as a medium for drama. Essentially unrhymed verse, blank verse had been used before on stage, by Peele and possibly by Kyd. But Marlowe became its master, using it in a sheer quantity and quality never before seen.

Marlowe also infused his dramas with a feeling of power and driving energy that had been lacking in the works of ear-lier playwrights. This was due in part to his technique of building each of his plots almost completely around a central char-acter, an individual whose exploits the audience followed with interest through-out. This was new to English drama; most earlier plays had tended to focus more or less equally on two or more characters. Even more significant, more often than not Marlowe's central characters are flawed heroes, sometimes called villain-heroes, each power hungry, treacherous, revengeful, or some combination of such negative traits. They are, says Thomas Parrott, "a group of villain-heroes or of strong men fighting, often in vain, against an overwhelming force." It is this sense of urgency, coupled with Marlowe's sensitivity as a poet, that makes these characters "passionate" and "real and living human beings, something other than the stiff figures of academic tragedy." This, Parrott continues, constitutes

the authentic gift of Marlowe. With all its faults and extravagance and careless work, Elizabethan drama [following Marlowe] is keenly sensitive to human passion and to its destructive effect upon the lives of men.[58]

It has been said that life and art imitate each other. And indeed, passion certainly had as much of a destructive effect on Marlowe's own life as it had on those of his characters. A vibrant, individualistic, feisty individual given to challenging authority, he often found himself on the wrong side of the law or social convention; and his violent temper and dangerous lifestyle ended up tragically cutting short one of history's more brilliant literary careers.

The Youthful Spy

Marlowe was born in Canterbury on February 6, 1564, making him Shakespeare's senior by a little more than two months. John Marlowe, the future playwright's father, was a prominent member of the local shoemakers' and tanners' guild, and the child's mother, Catherine Arthur, was the daughter of a Canterbury clergyman.

The primary school or schools young "Kit" Marlowe attended remain unknown.

Christopher Marlowe, one of the finest and most temperamental of the Elizabethan playwrights.

But evidence indicates he entered Canterbury's King's School in January 1579, when he was fifteen. Four years earlier, Matthew Parker, archbishop of Canterbury, had died and provided in his will for the establishment of three yearly scholarships for King's School graduates. These grants were intended to cover expenses at Corpus Christi College, at Cambridge (the same school Robert Greene attended), and it was understood that the boys who received them would go on to become clergymen. Having garnered one of these highly coveted scholarships, Marlowe enrolled at Cambridge in March 1581.

It did not take long for the high-strung young man to demonstrate that he was hardly clergyman material. In 1582, he began skipping school on a regular basis, and by the winter of 1584 he was absent more than half the time. This and other unacceptable behavior naturally upset the school authorities, and eventually his graduation and degree were in jeopardy. Yet Marlowe duly received his M.A. from Corpus Christi in July 1587. For a long time, scholars were perplexed about the young man's whereabouts during his long absences from school, as well as why the college overlooked them and awarded him his degree anyway.

At least a partial answer to these questions emerged in 1925 with the pioneering work of scholar J. Leslie Hotson. He discovered a highly revealing entry about Marlowe in the register of Queen Elizabeth's Privy Council. (The council

Young Marlowe benefited from a scholarship established by Matthew Parker (pictured here).

consisted of her personal and very powerful advisers, who oversaw national security of all kinds, from foreign threats to public morality.) Dated June 9, 1587, the entry reads:

Whereas it was reported that Christopher Marlowe was determined to [go] beyond the seas to Rheims and there to remain, Their Lordships thought it good to certify that he had no such intent, but that in all his actions he had behaved himself in [an] orderly and discreet [manner], whereby he had done her Majesty good service, and deserved to be rewarded for his faithful dealings. Their Lordships' request was that the rumor should be [ignored] . . . and that he should [receive his college] degree. . . . It is not her Majesty's pleasure that anyone employed as he had been, in matters touching the benefit of his country, should be defamed by those that are ignorant [of his whereabouts and actions].[59]

This extraordinary document first informs us that there had been rumors floating around Cambridge that Marlowe had intended to move to Rheims, in France. If so, it would have been a black mark against him. That city was then a major headquarters of English Roman Catholics, Elizabeth's enemies, and abandoning the Anglican Church for the Catholic cause would make the young man a traitor. However, Marlowe's trip "had no such intents," the queen's advisers asserted. He had "done her Majesty good service." As to what kind of service Marlowe had performed, the later phrase "in matters touching the benefit of his country" is apparently key. The consensus of modern scholars is that young Christopher Marlowe was an agent in the queen's secret service and that he had been regularly spying on Catholics and her other enemies. One can only speculate about the looks on the faces of the college officials when they received that stern message from the most powerful men in the land. This explains why the school caved in and granted the youth his degree without further ado.

Brushes with the Law

As for how Marlowe became involved in the espionage business to begin with, no one can say. What is more certain is that his ties to the inner circles of government remained in place in the years that followed and proved helpful in both his theatrical career and personal life. No sooner had he graduated from Cambridge when he acquired a wealthy patron, Sir Thomas Walsingham. Not only was Sir Thomas himself involved in the English spy network, he was also a kinsman of Sir Francis Walsingham, England's secretary of state and head of its intelligence service. Among the playwrights and poets for whom Thomas Walsingham already provided financial support were George Chapman and Thomas Watson; so it is not surprising that Marlowe became friendly with these writers, as well as with Thomas Nashe and others.

It was in the company of Thomas Watson that Marlowe had his first serious brush with the law. In September 1589, Marlowe got into a fight in an alley with a man named William Bradley, who had lately been threatening some sort of legal action against Watson. During the scuffle, Watson arrived and went to his friend's aid. When the fight ended Bradley was dead, and the authorities arrested both Marlowe and Watson on suspicion of murder and held them in Newgate Prison. (A rumor persists that while in Newgate

Queen Elizabeth shows a painting to Sir Francis Walsingham, whose brother Thomas, a high-ranking member of England's spy network, became Marlowe's patron.

Marlowe met notorious counterfeiter John Poole, who showed the playwright how to make both English and French coins.) Marlowe's and Watson's unusually swift release may have been the result of pressure from their patron and his high-placed associates. In any case, the police gave Marlowe a slap on the wrist and told him to stay out of trouble.

He did not follow this advice, however. In 1592, a London court summoned Marlowe to appear to answer charges of assaulting two constables in Shoreditch (in the eastern part of the city). The men were very shaken by the experience, claiming that the writer had nearly killed them. No evidence exists that Marlowe ever answered the charge, and once again his government connections appear to have shielded him. The secret service sent him to Rouen, in France, to aid its agents in supporting a group of Protestants against attack by Catholics.

In May of the following year, Marlowe was in trouble again, this time under arrest for suspicion of possessing anti-Christian documents. The authorities had first found them in the papers of playwright Thomas Kyd, with whom Marlowe had shared a room for a while; Kyd insisted that they belonged to Marlowe and had somehow gotten mixed in with his own manuscripts. This explanation seemed plausible because Marlowe had long been known for his "atheistic" sentiments and statements. It is important to note, however, as one scholar explains:

> Actually he was not an atheist in the proper sense; his writings clearly show that he believed in God. But he did indulge in a searching and irreverent criticism of both the Old and New Testaments, pointing out in jesting fashion some of their irrational inconsistencies, impossibilities, and absurdities—calling Moses, for instance, nothing but a "juggler" in performing his miracles. It was basically the institutions and beliefs of contemporary orthodox religion that he rejected.[60]

Whatever Marlowe's personal beliefs may have been, they were not enough to override his usefulness to the powers that be. Some evidence suggests that the Privy Council summoned and questioned him.

But unlike poor Kyd, Marlowe was neither imprisoned nor tortured and once again found himself free to go.

Taking the Town by Storm

In retrospect, Marlowe's secret, often seamy and dangerous personal life seems an odd backdrop to his short but brilliant theatrical-literary career. Even before leaving Cambridge, he had distinguished himself with a translation of the *Amores,* erotic expressions of love by the ancient Roman poet Ovid; a translation of the first book of the Roman epic poet Lucan's *Pharsalia;* and an original play, *Dido, Queen of Carthage,* also based on classical material.

These proved to be mere student exercises compared with Marlowe's professional creations. On reaching London in 1587, he scored an immediate hit with *Tamburlaine the Great* (in two parts), which he may have begun before graduating from Cambridge. Based on the life of the fourteenth-century Asian conqueror, Timur, the plot traces the title character's rise from an obscure shepherd to a mighty military leader who defeats the forces of Turkey, Syria, and Egypt. In staging the play, Marlowe marshaled a number of effective devices and resources. He centered the plot almost completely around Tamburlaine, endowing the work with power by focusing on a powerful man; and he gave the character strong, moving speeches in blank verse more vital and realistic than audiences were used to. In addition, he had the fortune

Tamerlane (or Tamburlaine) the Great was the title character of one of Marlowe's most popular plays.

of getting a major theatrical company—the Lord Admiral's Servants, featuring noted actor Edward Alleyn—to stage the work. Parrott writes:

> The novelty, the music of the verse, the acting and thunderous declamation [speaking style] of Alleyn, greatest actor of the day, took the town by storm. Marlowe's first play was epoch-making in the development of Elizabethan drama.[61]

In particular, Marlowe's heavy use of blank verse, with the placement of stresses and pauses varying from line to line, set a trend that other Elizabethan playwrights, including Shakespeare and Jonson, later followed. Adopting this style allowed Marlowe to avoid the often wooden, sing-song qualities of Kyd's lines, which are, as one critic has pointed out, "occasionally so monotonously regular that one is tempted to believe that sometimes he measured off the beats on his fingers."[62] Take, for example, the following lines from Kyd's *Spanish Tragedy:*

> Their violent shot resembling the ocean's rage,
>
> When, roaring loud and with swelling tide,
>
> It beats upon the ramparts of huge rocks,
>
> And gapes to swallow neighbor-bounding lands.[63]

By contrast, the beats and pauses in Marlowe's verses vary, imparting a more fluid, realistic quality, as in this tract from *Tamburlaine:*

> I that am termed the scourge and wrath of God,
>
> The only fear and terror of the world,
>
> Will first subdue the Turk and then enlarge
>
> Those Christian captives, which you keep as slaves.[64]

An engraving of the great actor Edward Alleyn, whose company staged Tamburlaine.

A String of Masterpieces

A combination of enormous talent, the proper connections, and fortunate timing had made Marlowe the most famous playwright in England at the tender age of twenty-three. Several other plays followed, each a masterpiece in its own right. *The Jew of Malta* (ca. 1589) introduced the concept of an unabashed villain as the leading character. (By today's standards, a ruthless conqueror like Tamburlaine would be considered a villain; but to the Elizabethans, such men were more often seen

as admirable for their strength and courage.) That leading character, Barabas, is a wealthy Jewish resident of the Mediterranean island of Malta. The island's scheming Christian governor confiscates Barabas's money, saying he will refund half if the Jew converts to Christianity. Barabas refuses this insulting offer and plots his revenge, which includes collaborating with invading Turks to overthrow the governor. Eventually the Jew becomes governor himself, but soon pays the price for his treachery by falling into a cauldron of boiling liquid.

The Jew of Malta is important literarily for several reasons. First, it was one of the first Elizabethan revenge plays written after the appearance of Kyd's *Spanish Tragedy;* second, in its portrayal of both Jews and Christians as disreputable schemers, *The Jew* was daring for a writer in a society in which Jews were distrusted and scorned and Christianity seen as the only true faith; and finally, the play's subject matter and characters influenced later English writers, including Shakespeare (especially in his *Merchant of Venice,* another play about a wealthy Jew).

Although the exact sequence and dating of Marlowe's plays remain uncertain, it appears that *The Jew* was followed by *The Tragicall History of Doctor Faustus* in 1590. The story of a man who sells his soul to the Devil, it weaves themes from the old morality plays (human temptation, fall from grace, and damnation) into a complex, mature, tragic framework. Next, probably, came *Edward II,* in 1591. Here, Marlowe transformed a simple historical chronicle about a weak king into a moving tragedy highlighted by realistic dialogue. The dramatist's last play, *The Massacre at Paris,* was composed in 1592 following his return from the siege of Rouen; unfortunately, only a badly mutilated version survives. Marlowe also turned out a long and very popular narrative poem—*Hero and Leander*—based on the famous tale of star-crossed lovers from classical mythology.

These are the works that can be definitely attributed to Marlowe. Over the years, various scholars have argued that he authored other plays, including one about the villainous English king Richard III and one or more parts of the *Henry VI* trilogy now viewed as belonging to Shakespeare. Some theorists have gone so far as to suggest that Marlowe *was* Shakespeare, that he did not die in 1593, but somehow survived, assumed a new identity, and went on to write the greatest plays in the English language.[65] However, no compelling evidence for this controversial claim has yet been advanced.

Marlowe's Mysterious Death

Much more speculation has surrounded the manner of Marlowe's confirmed death than his possible survival. Based on the limited reliable evidence available, the following scenario seems most likely. Only a few days after Marlowe had visited and been dismissed by the Privy Council (May 18, 1583), he traveled to the small village of Deptford, a few miles down the Thames from London. He may have been trying to avoid an outbreak of the plague that had just struck the city. On May 30, the playwright lingered for most of the day at Dame Elenor Bull's tavern, dining and drinking with three characters of bad reputation. Robert Poley was a former spy and ex-convict; Ingram Frizer, at the time still an agent in Walsingham's service, was

A nineteenth-century painting of the lovers Hero and Leander, subjects of one of Marlowe's poems.

known for shady financial dealings; and Nicholas Skeres was a known thief and shoplifter.

For reasons that are unclear, the four men got into a quarrel and Marlowe sprang up and attacked Frizer. Snatching the other man's own dagger, the playwright cut him twice, but Frizer managed to wrestle him to the floor. Frizer then turned the dagger toward his opponent, striking him just above the eye. The blade penetrated Marlowe's brain and he died instantly.

What were Marlowe and others doing in the tavern that day? And what was the cause of the argument and brawl that ended in the dramatist's untimely death? Numerous scholars and popular writers have attempted to answer these questions. Some have claimed that the meeting was purely social, the fight spontaneous, and that Frizer acted in self-defense. Others—most recently Charles Nicholl in his novel,

The Reckoning—have proposed that Marlowe was murdered in a nefarious plot involving the spy network he had long been part of.

Until such time, if ever, that any solid evidence emerges to shed new light on the matter, Marlowe's unfortunate death will remain a mystery. One thing seems clear. The passion for living, violent temper, and bent for risk taking that finally did him in were integral facets of the same rebellious nature that fueled his dramatic innovations. As scholar Philip Henderson puts it, Marlowe was

a master of stage-craft in the earlier days of the English drama—the pioneer from whose example those who followed profited most. . . . His life was as dangerous as his thought and, as much as he dared, he used the drama as a vehicle for his revolutionary conceptions.[66]

A Playwright for All Time: William Shakespeare

I n Shakespeare's great political play, *Julius Caesar,* a group of Roman senators stand over the bleeding body of Caesar the dictator, whom they have just slain. One of the leaders of the conspiracy, Cassius, says to the others, "How many ages hence shall this our lofty scene be acted over in states unborn and accents unknown!"[67] Here, the playwright showed that his character recognizes the enormity of the assassins' deed; in Cassius's view, Caesar's murder is an event of such epic proportions that it will be remembered by all future generations and reenacted often in their dramatic presentations. Indeed, as Shakespeare, with the benefit of hindsight, knew well, Cassius's prediction came true.

What Shakespeare perhaps did not foresee was how much that same idea might, in the fullness of time, be applied to himself and his own literary works. It is probable that when he died in 1616, he did not imagine that his plays would still be performed a century later, much less become, after *four* centuries, the most often performed, studied, and quoted of all dramatic works. Yet it did not take long for his contemporaries to realize the inevitability of his immortality. Only a scant seven years after his passing, his friend and rival playwright, Ben Jonson, recognized and acknowledged it. In the preface of the first major collection of Shakespeare's plays, the First Folio, Jonson called him "a monument without a tomb" and added: "He was not of an age, but for all time!"[68] Like Cassius's words spoken over Caesar, Jonson's over Shakespeare have proven prophetic. In the words of noted Harvard University scholar Harry Levin, Shakespeare's plays have been

> accorded a place in our culture above and beyond their topmost place in our literature. They have been virtually canonized as humanistic scriptures, the tested residue of pragmatic [practical] wisdom, a general collection of quotable texts and usable examples. Reprinted, reedited, commented upon, and translated into most languages, they have preempted more space on the library shelves than the books of—or about—any other author. Meanwhile, they have become a staple of the school and college curricula, as well as the happiest of hunting grounds for scholars and critics.[69]

The Evidence for Shakespeare's Life

Jonson, Levin, and countless others have eulogized Shakespeare as a poet for the ages. But what of Shakespeare the man in his own age, when he was but one of numerous playwrights competing in a cutthroat theatrical marketplace? The exact details of his life, especially his early years, are unknown. Yet the often voiced notion that Shakespeare led an almost totally mysterious and undocumented life

This nineteenth-century engraving shows William Shakespeare at work in his study.

(which has given rise to numerous vain attempts to prove that someone else wrote his plays) is a misconception. The fact is that for a common person of the Elizabethan period, Shakespeare's life was unusually *well* documented.

The evidence consists of over one hundred official documents, including entries about him and his relatives in parish registers and town archives, legal records involving property transfers, business letters to or about him, as well as his will. There are also more than fifty allusions to him and his works in the published writings of his contemporaries. The 1592 attack by rival dramatist Robert Greene is perhaps the most famous; another is a letter written to Shakespeare by Richard Quiney (a Stratford resident whose son wanted to marry the playwright's daughter Judith), bearing the address: "Deliver this letter to my loving good friend and countryman, Mr. William Shakespeare."[70] These sources do not tell us much about Shakespeare's personality, likes and dislikes, and personal beliefs. Yet they provide enough information to piece together a concise outline of the main events of his life.

Shakespeare was born in Stratford, now called Stratford-on-Avon, a village in Warwickshire County in central England, in 1564. The exact day is somewhat uncertain, but tradition accepts it as April 23. If this dating is indeed correct, it is an unusual coincidence, for April 23 is celebrated in England as St. George's Day, in honor of the country's patron

Shakespeare's birthplace and boyhood home in Stratford-on-Avon has been preserved. Every year thousands of tourists make the pilgrimage to Warwickshire to see it.

saint, and is also the documented month and day of Shakespeare's own death fifty-two years later. (The date of his christening is registered as April 26, 1564. Since it was then customary to baptize an infant no later than the first Sunday or holy day following its birth, most scholars favor April 22 or 23 as Shakespeare's birth date. Regarding the end of his life, the date of his burial is known—April 25, 1616; and when the burial customs of the time are considered, April 23 seems a likely date for his death.)

A Highly Rounded Education

It was by no means evident at first, however, that young Will Shakespeare would turn out to be a major contributor to and shaper of the new and growing Elizabethan theater. When he was born, his father, John Shakespeare, was a glove maker and perhaps also a wool and leather dealer in Stratford, which was far away from the bustling, cosmopolitan London, where most actors, writers, and other artists congregated and worked. The elder Shakespeare also held various local community positions, among them ale taster, town councilman, town treasurer, and eventually bailiff (mayor). John and his wife, Mary Arden, were married shortly before Queen Elizabeth ascended the English throne in 1558. And they subsequently produced eight children, of whom William was the third child and eldest son.

Scholars are reasonably certain that between the ages of seven and sixteen, Shakespeare attended Stratford's local grammar school. There, students studied Latin grammar and literature, including the works of the Roman writers Terence, Cicero, Virgil, and Ovid, as well as those of a few later European authors such as the Dutch moralist Erasmus. Following the educational customs of the day, Shakespeare and his classmates had to memorize the grammar and other information and then parrot it back when drilled by the schoolmaster. A rough idea of the process appears in the following scene from Shakespeare's *The Merry Wives of Windsor,* in which a parson (Evans) tests the Latin knowledge of a young boy (Will, a name unlikely to have been chosen by chance):

EVANS What is your genitive case plural, William?

WILL Genitive case?

EVANS Ay.

WILL *Horum, harum, horum.* . . .

EVANS Show me now, William, your declension of your pronouns.

WILL Forsooth [in truth], I have forgot.

EVANS It is *qui, quae, quod:* if you forget your *qui's,* your *quae's,* and your *quod's,* you must be preeches [whipped].[71]

In addition to these formal studies, Shakespeare must have done much reading on his own time when in his teens and twenties. We know this partly because his works reveal a knowledge not only of Latin, but also of French and several other languages. Shakespeare was also very well versed in both ancient and recent European history and fiction as well, including the classic works of Italy's Boccaccio and England's Chaucer. In addition, and perhaps most important, Shakespeare amassed a huge body of practical knowledge about life. In fact, says Shakespearean scholar John F. Andrews:

> Judging from his plays and poems, we may infer that Shakespeare was interested in virtually every aspect of human life—in professions such as law, medicine, religion, and teaching; in everyday occupations such as farming, sheepherding, tailoring, and shopkeeping; in skills such as fishing, gardening, and cooking. Much of what Shakespeare knew about these and countless other subjects he would have acquired from books. He must have been a voracious reader. But he would have learned a great deal, also, from simply being alert to all that went on around him.[72]

By his young adulthood, therefore, Shakespeare possessed an impressive, highly rounded education, most of it self-taught.

Why a Career in the Theater?

Putting aside informed speculation about Shakespeare's childhood and education, the first certain fact about him after his birth was his wedding, which his marriage license dates November 27, 1582. His bride, Anne Hathaway—the daughter of a farmer from the nearby village of Shottery—was eight years his senior. Local documents also reveal a daughter named Susanna, christened May 26, 1583, and twins, Hamnet and Judith,

This painting of Shakespeare likely dates from the early 1600s.

79

christened February 26, 1585. Other surviving records show that Hamnet died in 1596 at the age of eleven.

The exact reason that young Will Shakespeare chose the theater as a profession is unknown. But certain facts help to construct an educated guess, among them that companies of strolling actors visited and performed at Stratford periodically. For instance, Stratford records indicate such visits from the theatrical troupes The Queen's Men and The Earl of Worcester's Men in 1568 and 1569, when Shakespeare was about five. It may well be that traveling productions like these fascinated the young man enough to inspire his going to London to try his luck in the theater. Scholars believe that this event likely occurred in 1587, the year before the English victory over the Spanish Armada.

Concerning young Will Shakespeare's first professional job, various undocumented stories have survived. One maintains that he tended horses outside a theater until offered the position of assistant prompter (a stagehand who whispers lines to actors who have forgotten theirs). Scholars Gareth and Barbara Evans explain the two chief objections to this often-quoted tale:

The first is that there is no evidence whatsoever, and the second is that the Globe Theater was not built until 1599—ten years at least after Shakespeare arrived in London. . . . [There exists the] possibility that he

looked after horses at some other theater and that, after all, the early attachments of many of our eminent dramatists to their chosen profession have been no less menial.[73]

It is more likely, Shakespearean scholar François Laroque writes, that the young Shakespeare

attached himself to a theatrical company—perhaps the Queen's Men, which happened to have lost one of its members in a brawl. The young Shakespeare could easily have stepped into his shoes, as experience was not required. Actors learned on the job.[74]

Subsequent events suggest that the observant and talented Shakespeare learned quicker than most. By 1593 he had written *Richard III, The Comedy of Errors,* and *Henry VI, Parts 1, 2, and 3,* earning him a solid reputation as a playwright and actor in the London theater scene. At first, he did not attach himself exclusively to any specific theatrical company, but worked on and off with several, including that of Richard Burbage, the finest and most acclaimed actor of the time. Burbage, four years younger than Shakespeare, became the playwright's close friend and colleague and eventually played the title roles in the original productions of some of his greatest plays, including *Hamlet, Richard III, King Lear,* and *Othello.*

The great Sir Laurence Olivier as the evil King Richard III in Olivier's 1955 film version of the play. Shakespeare completed Richard III *in the early 1590s.*

London's theaters were closed during most of 1593 and 1594 because of a severe outbreak of the plague, and Shakespeare temporarily channeled his energies into writing pure poetry. Two long poems, *Venus and Adonis* and *Lucrece,* the only works he ever published himself, were completed in this interval and dedicated to his close friend, the earl of Southampton. (Some evidence has survived indicating that the earl lent the playwright money when he was low on funds during his early years in London.) These works established Shakespeare as an accepted and respectable literary figure; whereas his plays, like those of other playwrights of the time, were viewed as popular but lowbrow entertainment rather than as legitimate literature.

Achieving Success

Perhaps it was one of Southampton's loans (or maybe an outright gift) that allowed Shakespeare to purchase a modest share of a new theatrical company—The Lord Chamberlain's Men. Its founding in 1594 marked a crucial turning point in the playwright's career. Performing at all the major theaters of the day, including The Theatre, The Swan, and The Curtain (the famous Globe having not yet been built), the company thereafter provided Shakespeare with a ready creative outlet for his plays as well as a regular income. By 1603, when it became known as The King's Servants, it was performing periodically at the royal court, and Shakespeare was a major shareholder in all company profits.

As a permanent member of the company, Shakespeare had the opportunity to work on a regular basis with the best English actors of the day. In addition to the great Burbage, these included Henry Condell, John Heminge, William Sly, and Will Kempe. Kempe, one of the great comic players of the Elizabethan stage, specialized in broad, slapstick comedy and physical clowning. (Evidence suggests that he played the role of Peter, the bumbling servant to the Nurse in *Romeo and Juliet*, and Dogberry, the constable in *Much Ado About Nothing*.) Over the years Shakespeare wrote a number of comic roles especially for Kempe, among them Costard in *Love's Labor's Lost*, Launce in *The Two Gentlemen of Verona*, and Bottom in *A Midsummer Night's Dream*.

From 1594 on, in fact, Shakespeare devoted most of his time to writing plays, turning out a large number of astonishing

The Swan theater as it may have appeared in 1614. Before construction of The Globe, several of Shakespeare's plays were staged at The Swan.

In this scene from Henry V, *the title character attempts to win the heart of a French princess. The work was only one of several historical plays Shakespeare composed.*

variety and quality between 1594 and 1601. A mere partial list includes the comedies *The Merry Wives of Windsor, The Taming of the Shrew, The Two Gentlemen of Verona,* and *Twelfth Night;* the histories *Richard II, Henry IV, Parts 1 and 2,* and *Henry V;* and the tragedies *Julius Caesar, Romeo and Juliet,* and *Hamlet.* Not surprisingly, the playwright's reputation soared, as evidenced by the following 1598 remembrance by schoolmaster and schol-

ar Francis Meres (who died in 1647), praising his talent and skills:

The sweet witty soul of [the great ancient Roman poet] Ovid lives in mellifluous [smooth and sweet] and honey-tongued Shakespeare, witness his *Venis and Adonis,* his *Lucrece,* his . . . sonnets. . . . As [the Roman playwrights] Plautus and Seneca are accounted the best for Comedy and

Tragedy among the Latins: so Shakespeare among the English is the most excellent in both kinds for the stage.[75]

In spite of the grueling work schedule that must have been needed to turn out so many masterpieces in these years, the playwright somehow managed to find the time for journeys back and forth to rural Stratford and the family and community obligations centered there. In 1597 he became a local burgess (coun-cil member), by buying New Place, the largest and finest home in the town; the property included two barns and two gardens. Town records show that he later bought other property in the area, con-firming that he had by now acquired more than what was then viewed as a comfortable living.

A significant portion of this large income probably came from Shakespeare's one-eighth share in the profits of the new and very successful Globe theater, which opened in 1599. His colleagues

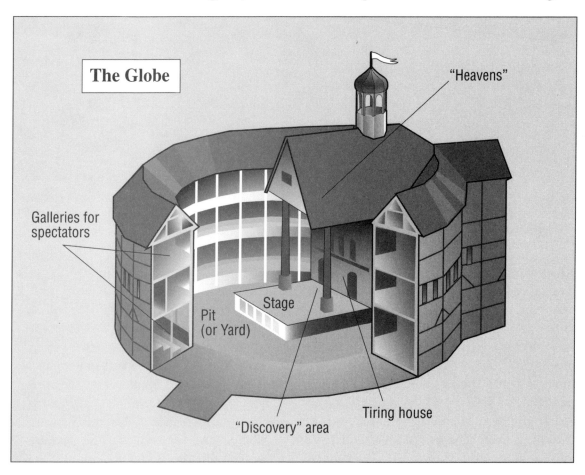

The Globe

"Heavens"

Galleries for spectators

Stage

Pit (or Yard)

"Discovery" area

Tiring house

Richard and Cuthbert Burbage had found it difficult to renew their lease at The Theatre playhouse (which their father had built in the London suburb of Shoreditch in 1576) and had decided to tear it down and erect their own playhouse. In the short span of eight months, they built The Globe on the south side of the Thames River, partly utilizing timbers and other materials from the recently demolished Theatre. It was for The Globe and the specific properties of its stage that Shakespeare tailored the plays he wrote in the years that followed. Between 1600 and 1607, the theater's yard (open-air central section) and platform (stage) were the scene of the premieres of most of what are now viewed as Shakespeare's greatest tragedies: *Hamlet, Othello, King Lear, Macbeth,* and *Antony and Cleopatra.*

His Literary Legacy

Only eight years separated the writing of these superb and timeless works and the playwright's untimely death. Evidently now secure in his fame and fortune, he appears to have spent much of his time during these final years at New Place in Stratford. There, according to various entries in local records and diaries, he became increasingly involved in community and family affairs. He still wrote plays, but no longer at the rapid pace he had maintained in his youth. His last works included *Coriolanus, Pericles, The Winter's Tale, Henry VIII,* and *The Two Noble Kinsmen,* all first performed between 1608 and 1613. *Kinsmen* turned out to be his swan song. He must have become seriously ill in March 1616, for his will was executed on March 25, and he died nearly a month later on April 23. The bulk of his estate went to his wife, sister, and daughters, Susanna and Judith, although he also left money to some of his theater colleagues, including Richard Burbage.

A few years after Shakespeare's death, a monument to him, designed by prosperous stonemason Gheerart (or Gerard) Janssen, was erected in Stratford Church. According to University of Maryland scholar Samuel Schoenbaum:

Janssen worked mainly in white marble, with black for the two Corinthian columns, and black touchstone for the inlaid panels. The columns support a cornice [horizontal molding] on which sit two small cherubic figures, both male; the left one, holding a spade, represents Labor; the right, with a skull and inverted torch, signifies Rest. They flank the familiar Shakespearean [coat of] arms, helm, and crest, carved in bas-relief on a square stone block. The design forms a pyramid at the apex [top] of which sits another skull. . . . Wearing a sleeveless gown over a doublet, Shakespeare stands with a quill pen in his right hand, a sheet of paper under his left, both hands resting on a cushion.[76]

Shakespeare received a greater posthumous honor in 1623 when two of his former theatrical partners, Henry Condell and John Heminge, published the so-called First Folio, a collection of the playwright's complete plays, under the title *Mr. William Shakespeare's Comedies, Histories, and Tragedies. Published According to the True Original Copies.* The exact nature of these "copies" that served as the Folio's basis remains unclear. Most scholars assume that they were various "quartos," early printed versions of the plays, which the actors often used as performance scripts.

Whatever its sources may have been, the First Folio was extremely important to posterity because it included eighteen plays that had not already been printed in quarto form and that might otherwise have been lost forever. Among them were some of the playwright's greatest works—*As You Like It, Macbeth, Antony and Cleopatra, The Tempest,* and *Julius Caesar.* Had only one of these masterpieces survived, it would surely rank its author as one of the leading Elizabethan playwrights. Combined with *Hamlet, Othello, King Lear, Twelfth Night, Richard III,* and the rest of

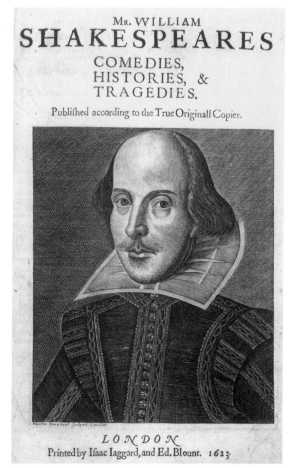

This likeness of Shakespeare from the title page of the First Folio was drawn by Martin Droeshout.

Shakespeare's output, it constitutes a literary legacy that has never been and may never again be matched.

Chapter 8

Shrewd Critic of Human Follies: Ben Jonson

To most people today who look back on the Elizabethan theater, the figure of William Shakespeare invariably looms as an overpowering presence, dwarfing most of his contemporaries. Modern scholars generally view Ben Jonson second in importance among these dramatists. Yet if one could travel back in time to London in that era, a surprise would be waiting. It would quickly become apparent that most of the Elizabethans themselves viewed Jonson as a more prominent literary figure than Shakespeare.

"The Tribe of Ben"

To understand this situation, it is necessary to consider the differences between the two men in their own day. First, Jonson had a longer career—about forty years, as compared with about twenty-five for Shakespeare. Jonson also led a more controversial life, which drew notoriety and commentary from nobles, politicians, writers, and literary critics; whereas the public knew relatively little about Shakespeare's private life, which was apparently more or less quiet and uneventful. So both circumstances and the passage of time established Jonson as the more distinctive social and theatrical character.

Also, although as a playwright Shakespeare certainly enjoyed a popular following in the public theaters, "serious" writers of philosophy, theology, and the natural sciences did not view his plays or those of other dramatists as worthy of being called literature. Many were never printed (and thereby lost), and when they *were* printed it was usually as an afterthought.

The younger, bolder Jonson challenged this state of affairs, insisting that his plays should be looked on as legitimate literature. And to emphasize the point, in 1616 he published a collection of his plays under the title *The Works of Benjamin Jonson*. Scholars and many oth-

This portrait of Ben Jonson is most often attributed to artist Isaac Oliver.

ers ridiculed his use of the word "Works," which they felt gave too much credit to mere plays. But Jonson ignored the critics; his careful oversight of both editing and presentation set new standards for the publication of plays and their acceptance as literature. In this way, his biographer David Riggs points out, he "created an 'authorized' text that could be shared again and again with an educated readership."[77] This example inspired friends of the now dead Shakespeare to collect and publish his plays seven years later in the First Folio, saving many as yet unpublished masterpieces for posterity.

In addition, unlike Shakespeare, Jonson developed a loyal following of young, highly educated playwrights and other writers who proudly came to call themselves "the tribe of Ben"; their works, as well as those of many later English writers, show his influence. In fact, Jonson actually saw himself as a sort of pioneer or reformer of the drama of his time. Specifically, he was deeply concerned that many plays lacked good form, followed few accepted literary rules, and were filled with boring clichés and lowbrow humor. In his view, as one modern scholar explains, most were

> badly written, stuffed with stale jokes and endless bombast [long declarative speeches], marred by obscenity and blasphemy . . . their plots were absurd, full of improbabilities and coincidences . . . their characters were incredible and there were too

many clowns . . . [and] they contained far too many violent, pointless, and noisy incidents—battles, storms, and shipwrecks, and so on.[78]

Jonson sought to establish, through the example of his own plays, correct rules for writing drama, especially for comedy, his forte. And in that regard he succeeded admirably. "No praise can be too high for the construction of his comedies," writes another of his biographers, J.B. Bamborough.

Nothing in them happens by chance and no "loose ends" are ever left dangling; it is not too much to say that every character who appears is given an intelligible motive for his actions, and his every entrance and exit is accounted for. Alongside the plays of [most of] his contemporaries, which often seem like heaps of broken parts, Jonson's plays resemble well-oiled, smoothly-running machines.[79]

The Reluctant Bricklayer

Jonson's path to the position of preeminent dramatist of his day was long and strewn with obstacles that would surely have deterred men of lesser ambition and talent. About a month before his birth— in London in June 1572—his father, a minister whose name is unknown, died. This apparently left the family destitute; so young Ben's mother, whose name likewise has not survived, wasted no time in finding a second husband. The stepfather, whose name may have been Robert Brett, was a successful bricklayer who, as a matter of course, expected the boy to become an apprentice in that profession.

Even as a child, however, Jonson, who must have been a good deal smarter and more sensitive than the average boy, had no desire to become a laborer. Luckily for him, when he was seven a family friend, whose identity is unknown, helped enroll him in the prestigious Westminster School. There, his schoolmaster was William Camden, one of the leading educators and scholars in all England. Thanks to Camden, Jonson gained a strong foundation in and love for fine literature that stayed with him the rest of his life.

Whoever Jonson's financial mentor was, he could not or would not provide the necessary monies for him to attend college. And since the family could not afford to help, the young man was forced to leave school at age sixteen. He reluctantly took a job building masonry walls with his stepfather. But as Jonson later recalled, he "could not endure"[80] this avocation and ran away and joined the British army. In a military campaign in the Netherlands, he saw action and killed an enemy soldier in hand-to-hand combat.

First Foray into the Theater

Exactly when Jonson returned to London from the service is uncertain. The next documented incident in his life was his marriage in November 1594 to a young woman named Anne Lewis. Supporting a wife required an income, of course; but there were few respectable career opportunities for a young man without a college degree who also rejected the idea of manual labor. Perhaps this was his motivation for becoming an actor with a group of strolling players that same year. Contemporary playwright Thomas Dekker later claimed that Jonson played the lead role in Kyd's *Spanish Tragedy*. The company was likely the Earl of

The Westminster School in London as it appeared in 1930. Jonson studied there under William Camden, one of the leading English educators of the day.

Pembroke's Men, since evidence shows that that group performed Kyd's play on a 1595–1596 tour.

In the summer of 1597, Jonson encountered his biggest obstacle yet—a jail term. He clearly felt he was destined to be a dramatist and had found an opportunity to make the transition from acting to writing, namely finishing a play (*The Isle of Dogs*) begun by Thomas Nashe. The play opened at The Swan in July. But the authorities felt its content was offensive, closed it down, and arrested the actors, as well as Jonson. Released from prison in October, the aspiring writer had to borrow money to make ends meet.

Refusing to be defeated, Jonson persevered, wrote another play, and this time scored big. In 1598, *Every Man in His Humor,* a comedy, peaked the interest of The Lord Chamberlain's Men, the company partially owned by Shakespeare. Jonson had the thrill and honor of seeing the work performed that year, with Shakespeare and renowned actors Richard Burbage and Will Kempe all taking roles.

Every Man in His Humor remains one of Jonson's finest plays and exemplifies his approach to comedy, which was then fairly unique. He summed up his theory in the prologue (added later), in which he expresses the hope that the audience will be pleased to see a funny play without a lot of violence and special effects. No chorus of actors would wax eloquent to "waft you over the seas," he said, nor would a loud drum be played "to tell you when the storm doth come." Instead, his comedy would "show an image of the times, and sport with human follies, not with crimes." In other words, he would poke fun at everyday human foibles—"I mean such errors as you'll all confess; by laughing at them, they deserve no less."[81] These follies, displayed by the characters as they make their way through a series of zany twists and turns reminiscent of those in television situation comedies, include excessive jealousy, conceit, suspicion, and stupidity.

Imprisoned Again

No sooner had Jonson made a name for himself when he once more found himself in trouble. This time he got into a duel with and killed another actor, Gabriel Spencer, a former member of Pembroke's Men. The jury at Jonson's trial gave the following synopsis of events:

[Jonson] made an assault with force and arms, etc., against and upon . . . Gabriel Spencer . . . at Shoreditch . . . and with a certain sword of iron and steel . . . of the price of three shillings . . . feloniously and willfully struck and beat the same Gabriel, then and there with the aforesaid sword, giving . . . Gabriel's right side a mortal wound, of the depth of six inches and the breadth of one inch, of which mortal wound the same Gabriel Spencer then and there died instantly.[82]

Jonson's expression in this portrait captures a mixture of keen intelligence and anxiety over his troubled life.

unpopular in England at this time and were often the targets of hatred and persecution. "Catholics who declined to attend Anglican services," Riggs explains,

incurred a fine of twenty pounds a month [a very large sum at the time] and if they were unable to pay it, their property was confiscated. They could not hold public office. It was a felony to receive a priest and . . . a felony to take the sacrament [Holy Communion] from him. Catholics were subject to arbitrary imprisonment and excruciating tortures at the hands of their captors; those suspected of plotting against the crown could expect to have their intestines removed in public.[83]

Jonson was found guilty and imprisoned. Luckily, he managed to escape the death penalty by falling back on an archaic law that allowed male felons who were literate to have their cases referred to a bishop's court. In Jonson's case, the judge asked him to translate a passage from a Latin Bible, and when he did so with ease, the authorities freed him.

For some reason, while in prison Jonson converted to Catholicism. It is difficult to understand why he would do so, considering that he desired to continue a very visible career in the public theater. After all, Catholics were extremely

Whatever the playwright's reasons for becoming a Catholic, his conversion irritated the authorities, who kept watch on him and later pressured him to attend Anglican services.

At the Top of His Form

After his release, Jonson was penniless again. Hoping to make money, he turned out another comedy—*Every Man Out of His Humor*—which The Lord Chamberlain's Men staged at the new Globe theater in 1599. This was not as well received as *Every Man In,* however, so he tried his hand at writing for the boys' schools. About 1600, the Boys of St. Paul's Choir staged his *Cynthia's Revels,* a fantasy set in the court of Cynthia, the moon goddess. With its mythological framework and tribute to the queen through the character of Cynthia, it was reminiscent of Lyly's *Endymion.*

The following year Jonson received an invitation from the master of revels to present *Cynthia's Revels* for Queen Elizabeth. The piece did not go over well at court, though, because the author, in his usual attempt to expose human follies, referred to courtiers as arrogant and ignorant. Jonson was much more successful as a court writer after Elizabeth's death in 1603. For her successor, James I, and his queen, the playwright composed several masques, light entertainments combining acting, singing, and dancing. These included *The Masque of Blackness* (1605), *Hue and Cry After Cupid* (1608), and *The Masque of Queens* (1609).

Jonson did not abandon the public theater, however. Between 1606 and 1614 he was at the top of his form and turned out most of his greatest plays—*Volpone, Epicoene, The Alchemist,* and *Bartholomew Fair.* All of these comedies, like *Every Man In,* express his marked dislike of human vice and excess and his delight in exposing them. The characters who demonstrate these vices are often made to look ridiculous; but the author draws them in such detail that they become almost realistic portraits of the people and habits of his age. This careful attention to detail remains one of the most enduring strengths of these works. Thomas Parrott elaborates:

[Jonson's] comedies are invaluable social documents, since they present an unequalled picture of life in England during the great Elizabethan Age. To take one example out of many, Shakespeare never so much as mentions the new fashion of smoking; Jonson's comedies are [filled with references to] the pipe. Tobacco may be trivial, but there is more than smoke in Jonson's plays. There is not a folly, an affectation, or a fraud of his day that is not castigated [severely criticized] by his satire; it ranges from new fashions in dress and speech to the proposed transmutation [transformation] of base metals into gold and to grandiose schemes for reclaimed drowned lands. And all this matter is presented in "language such as men do use," in prose for the most part, or in verse that has little of the [flowery artificial style] of poetry.[84]

The Twilight of Elizabethan Drama

After a long period of critical and financial success and few if any personal problems, to his dismay Jonson suddenly began to experience setbacks. In 1623, his entire library, collected over the course of his adult life, was destroyed in

In this photo from a modern production of Volpone, *two ambitious relatives hover over the dying title character. Jonson reveled in exposing greed and other human vices.*

a fire. Two years later, his longtime patron, James I, died. That monarch's son, Charles I, was cool toward the dramatist, who was no longer asked to supply masques for the royal court. Compounding matters, the playwright suffered a stroke in 1628 and was thereafter confined to his home. He continued to write plays from his bed; but they were not nearly as incisive and successful as those penned in his prime. After a second stroke, on August 6, 1637, Jonson died, lonely and debt-ridden. He was buried not far from his old friend Will Shakespeare in Poet's Corner, that special section of Westminster Abbey set aside for England's most beloved literary figures.

Despite Jonson's considerable talents and contributions to Elizabethan drama in its fading twilight, Shakespeare's star eventually rose higher than his in the literary firmament. Jonson was certainly as smart, educated, and ingenious as his rival. Yet his corpus of plays does not come close to matching Shakespeare's in sheer size and variety, not to mention poetic beauty, emotional power, and insight into the human condition. The great seventeenth-century English dramatist John Dryden echoed the judgment of later generations when he said:

If I would compare [Jonson] with Shakespeare, I must acknowledge him the more correct poet, but Shakespeare the greater wit. Shakespeare was the Homer [the ancient Greek author of the epic poems the *Iliad* and the *Odyssey*], or father of our dramatic poets; Jonson was the Virgil [the ancient Roman author of the epic poem the *Aeneid*], the pattern of elaborate writing. I admire him, but I *love* Shakespeare.[85]

Another way to phrase it would be that Jonson was the epitome of style

Jonson was buried in Poet's Corner, one of the most famous parts of London's Westminster Abbey. Other writers interred there include William Shakespeare, John Dryden, and Charles Dickens.

and Shakespeare of substance; and it is only human nature to prefer substance over style. Yet it must not be forgotten that these two men and the other major Elizabethan playwrights, whatever the size of their individual contributions, often influenced and helped to shape one another's style and substance. And it is only right to acknowledge that the best among them would not have attained the greatness he did without the others. Perhaps, therefore, it is better to remember them collectively, as members of a special and remarkable group. In noted scholar James Shapiro's words, "Rivals with each other, it is fair to say that they have not been rivaled since."[86]

Notes

Introduction—Birth of the English-Speaking Theater

1. Thomas M. Parrott and Robert H. Ball, *A Short View of Elizabethan Drama*. New York: Scribner's, 1958, p. 63.
2. Parrott and Ball, *Short View of Elizabethan Drama*, p. 63.

Chapter 1—"On Your Imaginary Forces Work": The Elizabethan Theater

3. Karl J. Holzknecht, *The Backgrounds of Shakespeare's Plays*. New York: American Book Company, 1950, pp. 33–34.
4. Quoted in Ivor Brown, *How Shakespeare Spent the Day*. New York: Hill and Wang, 1963, p. 154.
5. A.A. Mendilow, "The Elizabethan Theater," in A. A. Mendilow and Alice Shalvi, *The World and Art of Shakespeare*. New York: Daniel Davey, 1967, pp. 26–27.
6. Michael Hattaway, *Elizabethan Popular Theater: Plays in Performance*. London: Routledge and Kegan Paul, 1982, p. 13.
7. Ronald Watkins, *On Producing Shakespeare*. New York: Benjamin Blom, 1964, pp. 18–20.

8. William Shakespeare, *Henry V*, act 1, scene 1, lines 11–28.
9. Quoted in Hattaway, *Elizabethan Popular Theater*, p. 86.
10. Quoted in Hattaway, *Elizabethan Popular Theater*, p. 86.
11. Shakespeare, *Hamlet*, act 3, scene 2, lines 38–43.
12. G.B. Harrison, *The Story of Elizabethan Drama*. Cambridge: Cambridge University Press, 1969, pp. 94–95.
13. Brown, *How Shakespeare Spent the Day*, p. 14.

Chapter 2—The Courtly Dreamer: John Lyly

14. Parrott and Ball, *Short View of Elizabethan Drama*, p. 65.
15. Quoted in John Dover Wilson, *John Lyly*. New York: Haskell House, 1970, p. 6. It should be noted that Harvey strongly disliked Lyly and therefore may have exaggerated.
16. Quoted in Wilson, *John Lyly*, pp. 11–12.
17. Quoted in G.K. Hunter, *Lyly and Peele*. London: Longman, Green, 1968, p. 19.
18. Joseph W. Houppert, *John Lyly*. Boston: Twayne, 1975, p. 16.

19. Wilson, *John Lyly*, p. 17.

20. Wilson, *John Lyly*, p. 98.

21. John Lyly, *Endymion,* act. 5, scene 3, lines 255–262, in Arthur H. Nethercot et al., eds., *Elizabethan Plays.* New York: Holt, Rinehart, and Winston, 1971, p. 217.

22. Lyly, *Endymion,* act. 1, scene 1, lines 43–58, Nethercot et al., *Elizabethan Plays,* p. 184.

23. Wilson, *John Lyly*, p. 127.

24. Quoted in Nethercot et al., *Elizabethan Plays,* p. 180.

25. Wilson, John *Lyly,* p. 3.

Chapter 3—Father of the Revenge Tragedy: Thomas Kyd

26. Quoted in Nethercot et al., *Elizabethan Plays,* p. 328.

27. Philip Edwards, *Thomas Kyd and Early Elizabethan Tragedy.* London: Longman Group, 1966, p. 6.

28. Parrott and Ball, *Short View of Elizabethan Drama,* pp. 76–77.

29. Harrison, *Story of Elizabethan Drama,* p. 23.

30. Norrie Epstein, *The Friendly Shakespeare: A Thoroughly Painless Guide to the Best of the Bard.* New York: Viking Penguin, 1993, p. 308.

31. William Shakespeare, *Hamlet,* First Quarto, act 3, scene 4.

32. Thomas Kyd, *The Spanish Tragedy,* act 4, scene 1, lines 46–49, in Nethercot et al., *Elizabethan Plays,* p. 377.

33. Frederick S. Boas, ed., *The Works of Thomas Kyd.* Oxford: Clarendon Press, 1967, pp. liii–liv.

Chapter 4—Poet of Pageant and Drama: George Peele

34. Leonard R.N. Ashley, *George Peele.* New York: Twayne, 1970, first page of preface.

35. Ashley, *George Peele,* p. 168.

36. Ashley, *George Peele,* p. 41.

37. George Peele, *The Arraignment of Paris,* act 5, scene 1, lines 70–81, in Nethercot et al., *Elizabethan Plays,* p. 240.

38. Thomas Campbell, *An Essay on English Poetry,* quoted in Ashley, *George Peele,* p. 152.

39. Peele, *The Love of King David and Fair Bethsabe,* scene 1, lines 92–95, 102–104, quoted in Hunter, *Lyly and Peele,* p. 42.

40. Quoted in Ashley, *George Peele,* p. 174.

41. Quoted in Ashley, *George Peele,* p. 169.

42. Quoted in Ashley, *George Peele,* p. 37.

43. Quoted in Nethercot et al., *Elizabethan Plays,* p. 217.

44. Quoted in Nethercot et al., *Elizabethan Plays,* p. 217.

Chapter 5—A Man at War Within Himself: Robert Greene

45. Thomas Nashe, "Strange News of Intercepting Certain Letters," quot-

ed in Nicholas Storojenko, *Robert Greene: His Life and Works.* trans. E.A. Brayley Hodgetts, in Alexander Grosart, ed., *The Life and Complete Works in Prose and Verse of Robert Greene*, vol. 1. New York: Russell and Russell, 1964, p. 19.

46. William A. Neilson, ed., *Chief Elizabethan Dramatists Excluding Shakespeare.* New York: Houghton Mifflin, 1911, p. 870.

47. From Robert Greene's *Repentance,* quoted in Nethercot et al., *Elizabethan Plays,* p. 261.

48. Quoted in Nethercot et al., *Elizabethan Plays,* p. 261.

49. Quoted in Nethercot et al., *Elizabethan Plays,* p. 261.

50. Quoted in Nethercot et al., *Elizabethan Plays,* p. 261.

51. Quoted in Nethercot et al., *Elizabethan Plays,* pp. 261–62.

52. Robert Greene, *The Honorable History of Friar Bacon and Friar Bungay,* scene 11, lines 116–27, in Nethercot et al., *Elizabethan Plays,* p. 294.

53. J.M. Brown, "An Early Rival of Shakespeare," quoted in Grosart, *Life and Complete Works in Prose and Verse of Robert Greene,* vol. 1, p. xvi.

54. Storojenko, *Robert Greene,* in Grosart, *Life and Complete Works in Prose and Verse of Robert Greene,* vol. 1, pp. 228–29.

55. Quoted in G. Blakemore Evans and J.J.M. Tobin, gen. eds., *The Riverside Shakespeare.* Boston: Houghton Mifflin, 1974, p. 1,835.

56. Brown, "An Early Rival of Shakespeare," in Grosart, *Life and Complete Works in Prose and Verse of Robert Greene,* vol. 1, pp. xvi–xvii.

57. Quoted in Storojenko, *Robert Greene,* in Grosart, *Life and Complete Works in Prose and Verse of Robert Greene,* vol. 1, p. 54.

Chapter 6—Risk Taker and Mystery Maker: Christopher Marlowe

58. Parrott and Ball, *Short View of Elizabethan Drama,* pp. 90–91.

59. Quoted in Nethercot et al., *Elizabethan Plays,* p. 434.

60. Quoted in Nethercot, *Elizabethan Plays,* pp. 435–36.

61. Parrott and Ball, *Short View of Elizabethan Drama,* p. 81.

62. Harrison, *Story of Elizabethan Drama,* p. 26.

63. Kyd, *Spanish Tragedy,* act 1, scene 2, lines 48–51, in Nethercot et al., *Elizabethan Plays,* pp. 337–38.

64. Christopher Marlowe, *Tamburlaine the Great, Part 1,* act 3, scene 3, lines 44–47, in Nethercot et al., *Elizabethan Plays,* p. 462.

65. The most prominent example is Calvin Hoffman, *The Murder of the Man Who Was Shakespeare.* New York: Messner, 1955.

66. Philip Henderson, *Christopher Marlowe.* London: Longman Group, 1972, p. 37.

Chapter 7—A Playwright for All Time: William Shakespeare

67. Shakespeare, *Julius Caesar*, act 3, scene 1, lines 113–15.
68. Quoted in Evans and Tobin, *Riverside Shakespeare*, pp. 65–66.
69. Harry Levin, "General Introduction," in Evans and Tobin, *Riverside Shakespeare*, p. 1.
70. Quoted in B.R. Lewis, *The Shakespeare Documents*. New York: Oxford University Press, 1940–1941, vol. 1, p. 226.
71. Shakespeare, *The Merry Wives of Windsor*, act 4, scene 1, lines 57–61, 74–78.
72. John F. Andrews, "The Past Is Prologue," in Wim Coleman, ed., *Othello*. Logan, IA: Perfection Forms Company, 1987, pp. viii–ix.
73. Gareth and Barbara Lloyd Evans, *The Shakespeare Companion*. New York: Scribner's, 1978, p. 21.
74. François Laroque, *The Age of Shakespeare*. New York: Harry N. Abrams, 1993, p. 39.
75. Quoted in "Life of Shakespeare," in Mendilow and Shalvi, *World and Art of Shakespeare*, p. 9.
76. Samuel Schoenbaum, *William Shakespeare: A Compact Documentary Life*. New York: Oxford University Press, 1977, p. 308.

Chapter 8—Shrewd Critic of Human Follies: Ben Jonson

77. David Riggs, *Ben Jonson: A Life*. Cambridge, MA: Harvard University Press, 1989, p. 221.
78. J.B. Bamborough, *Ben Jonson*. London: Longman Group, 1971, p. 9.
79. Bamborough, *Ben Jonson*, pp. 10–11.
80. Quoted in Riggs, *Ben Jonson*, p. 19.
81. Ben Jonson, *Every Man in His Humor*, prologue, lines 15–28, in C.F. Tucker Brooke and Nathaniel B. Paradise, eds., *English Drama, 1580–1642*. Boston: D.C. Heath, 1933, p. 437.
82. Quoted in Riggs, *Ben Jonson*, p. 49.
83. Riggs, *Ben Jonson*, p. 51.
84. Parrott and Ball, *Short View of Elizabethan Drama*, p. 150.
85. Quoted in James Shapiro, *Rival Playwrights: Marlowe, Jonson, Shakespeare*. New York: Columbia University Press, 1991, p. 163.
86. Shapiro, *Rival Playwrights*, p. 170.

For Further Reading

Michael Bender, *All the World's a Stage: A Pop-Up Biography of William Shakespeare*. San Francisco: Chronicle Books, 1999. A colorful introduction to Shakespeare's life and accomplishments for basic readers.

Peter Chrisp, *Welcome to the Globe: The Story of Shakespeare's Theater.* London: Dorling Kindersley, 2000. Eye-catching color illustrations adorn this excellent reconstruction of The Globe, one of the chief theaters in London during the Elizabethan Age. Aimed at young readers.

Laura K. Egendorf, *Elizabethan Drama*. San Diego: Greenhaven Press, 2000. A very useful compilation of information about Elizabethan plays and playwrights for high school and general, nonscholarly readers.

Don Nardo, ed., *Readings on Romeo and Juliet*. San Diego: Greenhaven Press, 1998. This collection of essays about one of Shakespeare's best-loved plays covers the playwright's life and times as well as the play's themes, characters, and literary merits. The reading level is high school and up.

————, *Understanding Hamlet*. San Diego: Lucent Books, 2001. An easy-to-read but highly detailed and informative overview of what many have called the greatest play ever written by the greatest playwright who ever lived, including thorough discussions of the plot, characters, themes, performance history, and more. Highly recommended.

Charles Nicholl, *The Reckoning: The Murder of Christopher Marlowe*. Chicago: University of Chicago Press, 1995. This extremely well researched novel attempts to reconstruct the circumstances surrounding the violent death of Marlowe, one of the finest of the Elizabethan playwrights. Utilizing many colorful characters, including William Shakespeare, and placing them in realistic Elizabethan settings, Nicholl makes the case that Marlowe was murdered.

Diane Yancey, *Life in the Elizabethan Theater*. San Diego: Lucent Books, 1997. A well-written overview of Elizabethan theaters, actors, playwrights, audiences, and so forth. Highly recommended.

Major Works Consulted

John C. Adams, *The Globe Playhouse: Its Design and Equipment*. Cambridge, MA: Harvard University Press, 1942. An indispensable mine of information about the theater used by Shakespeare and his colleagues and how it looked and operated.

Gerald E. Bentley, *Shakespeare: A Biographical Handbook*. Westport, CT: Greenwood, 1986. Contains much valuable information about Shakespeare, his plays, and his society.

Max Bluestone and Norman Rabkin, eds., *Shakespeare's Contemporaries*. Englewood Cliffs, NJ: Prentice-Hall, 1970. A very useful scholarly study of various Elizabethan playwrights, including John Lyly, George Peele, Robert Greene, Thomas Kyd, Christopher Marlowe, Thomas Dekker, Thomas Heywood, Ben Jonson, George Chapman, John Ford, and others. Highly recommended for devotees of the subject.

Philip Edwards, *Thomas Kyd and Early Elizabethan Tragedy*. London: Longman Group, 1966. An informative book that tells what is known about Kyd's life and summarizes his accomplishments and importance as a playwright.

Norrie Epstein, *The Friendly Shakespeare: A Thoroughly Painless Guide to the Best of the Bard*. New York: Viking Penguin, 1993. One of the best available general introductions to Shakespeare, his works, and his times.

Richard Harp and Stanley Stewart, eds., *The Cambridge Companion to Ben Jonson*. Cambridge: Cambridge University Press, 2000. An excellent general overview of Jonson's life, writings, and literary influence.

G.B. Harrison, *Elizabethan Plays and Players*. Ann Arbor: University of Michigan Press, 1956. Harrison, one of the leading Elizabethan theater scholars of the twentieth century, delivers a first-rate overview of some of the more important aspects of the subject.

———, *The Story of Elizabethan Drama*. Cambridge: Cambridge University Press, 1969. In this short but well-informed book, Harrison briefly discusses the importance of Thomas Kyd and *The Spanish Tragedy,* as well as the major works of Marlowe, Greene, Shakespeare, and Jonson.

Michael Hattaway, *Elizabethan Popular Theater: Plays in*

Performance. London: Routledge and Kegan Paul, 1982. A scholarly but readable study of Elizabethan theaters and actors.

Karl J. Holzknecht, *The Backgrounds of Shakespeare's Plays*. New York: American Book Company, 1950. An excellent source of information about the derivation of Shakespeare's plots, as well as about how the plays were presented.

Lisa Hopkins, *Christopher Marlowe: A Literary Life*. New York: St. Martin's Press, 2000. In this excellent new book, Hopkins discusses some of Marlowe's hallmarks, including his keen ability to depict foreign settings and his opposition to many of the accepted religious and sexual conventions of his day, as well as his lasting literary influence.

W. David Kay, *Ben Jonson: A Literary Life*. Hampshire, UK: Palgrave, 1995. A very useful overview of Jonson and his importance as a playwright.

François Laroque, *The Age of Shakespeare*. New York: Harry N. Abrams, 1993. A short, entertaining sketch of Shakespeare's life and times, enhanced by many beautiful color drawings and photos.

Peter Levi, *The Life and Times of William Shakespeare*. New York: Henry Holt, 1989. One of the better Shakespeare biographies, written by a noted scholar (who has also penned a number of important books about the ancient Greeks and Romans).

B.R. Lewis, *The Shakespeare Documents*. 2 vols. New York: Oxford University Press, 1940–1941. Long recognized as the most complete compilation of original documents pertaining to Shakespeare and his immediate associates and friends.

Arthur H. Nethercot et al, eds., *Elizabethan Plays*. New York: Holt, Rinehart, and Winston, 1971. A fulsome collection of Elizabethan plays, including selections by Thomas Preston, John Lyly, George Peele, Robert Greene, Thomas Kyd, Christopher Marlowe, Thomas Dekker, George Chapman, John Marston, and Thomas Heywood, along with considerable biographical information about each of these men.

Peter Quennell, *Shakespeare: A Biography*. Cleveland: World Publishing, 1963. This well-written synopsis of Shakespeare's life and work is by one of the most widely respected Shakespearean scholars.

John Dover Wilson, *John Lyly*. New York: Haskell House, 1970. One of the greatest of all Elizabethan/Shakespearean scholars delivers an information-packed, thoughtful discussion of Lyly's life and works. Highly recommended for fans of Elizabethan drama.

Additional Works
Consulted

Leonard R.N. Ashley, *George Peele*. New York: Twayne, 1970.

Isaac Asimov, *Asimov's Guide to Shakespeare*. New York: Avenel Books, 1978.

J.B. Bamborough, *Ben Jonson*. London: Longman Group, 1971.

Alfred Bates, ed., *The Drama: Its History, Literature, and Influence on Civilization*. Vol. 13. New York: AMS Press, 1970.

Frederick S. Boas, ed., *The Works of Thomas Kyd*. Oxford: Clarendon Press, 1967.

Charles Boyce, *Shakespeare: A to Z: The Essential Reference to His Plays, His Poems, His Life and Times, and More*. New York: Facts On File, 1990.

Andrew C. Bradley, *Shakespearean Tragedy*. New York: Viking Penguin, 1991.

C.F. Tucker Brooke and Nathaniel B. Paradise, eds. *English Drama, 1580–1642*. Boston: D.C. Heath, 1933.

Ivor Brown, *How Shakespeare Spent the Day*. New York: Hill and Wang, 1963.

———, *Shakespeare and the Actors*. New York: Coward McCann, 1970.

Marchette Chute, *Shakespeare of London*. New York: E.P. Dutton, 1949.

Wim Coleman, ed., *Othello*. Logan, IA: Perfection Forms Company, 1987.

Gareth and Barbara Lloyd Evans, *The Shakespeare Companion*. New York: Scribner's, 1978.

G. Blakemore Evans and J.J.M. Tobin, gen. eds., *The Riverside Shakespeare*. Boston: Houghton Mifflin, 1974.

Harley Granville-Barker and G.B. Harrison, eds., *A Companion to Shakespeare Studies*. Cambridge: Cambridge University Press, 1959.

Philip Henderson, *Christopher Marlowe*. London: Longman Group, 1972.

Calvin Hoffman, *The Murder of the Man Who Was Shakespeare*. New York: Messner, 1955.

Joseph W. Houppert, *John Lyly*. Boston: Twayne, 1975.

G.K. Hunter, *Lyly and Peele*. London: Longman, Green, 1968.

Ben Jonson, *Every Man in His Humor*. Ed. Robert S. Miola. Manchester, UK: Manchester University Press, 2000.

Thomas Kyd, *The Spanish Tragedy*.

Ed. David M. Bevington. Manchester, UK: Manchester University Press, 1998.

François Laroque, *Shakespeare's Festive World: Elizabethan Seasonal Entertainment and the Professional Stage*. New York: Cambridge University Press, 1991.

Christopher Marlowe, *Tamburlaine the Great*. Ed. J.S. Cunningham. Manchester, UK: Manchester University Press, 1998.

A.A. Mendilow and Alice Shalvi, *The World and Art of Shakespeare*. New York: Daniel Davey, 1967.

William A. Neilson, ed., *Chief Elizabethan Dramatists Excluding Shakespeare*. New York: Houghton Mifflin, 1911.

Thomas M. Parrott and Robert H. Ball, *A Short View of Elizabethan Drama*. New York: Scribner's, 1958.

Michael Pincombe, ed., *The Plays of John Lyly: Eros and Eliza*. Manchester, UK: Manchester University Press, 1997.

David Riggs, *Ben Jonson: A Life*. Cambridge, MA: Harvard University Press, 1989.

Pat Rogers, ed., *The Oxford Illustrated History of English Literature*. New York: Oxford University Press, 1987.

A.L. Rowse, *Shakespeare the Man*. New York: Harper and Row, 1973.

Samuel Schoenbaum, *William Shakespeare: A Compact Documentary Life*. New York: Oxford University Press, 1977.

James Shapiro, *Rival Playwrights: Marlowe, Jonson, Shakespeare*. New York: Columbia University Press, 1991.

Simon Shepherd, *Marlowe and the Politics of Elizabethan Theater*. New York: St. Martin's Press, 1986.

Arthur C. Sprague, *Shakespeare and the Actor's Stage Business in His Plays (1660–1905)*. Cambridge, MA: Harvard University Press, 1944.

Nicholas Storojenko, *Robert Greene: His Life and Works*. Trans. E.A. Brayley Hodgetts, in Alexander Grosart, ed., *The Life and Complete Works in Prose and Verse of Robert Greene*, vol. 1. New York: Russell and Russell, 1964.

Clarice Swisher, ed., *Readings on the Tragedies of William Shakespeare*. San Diego: Greenhaven Press, 1996.

Ronald Watkins, *On Producing Shakespeare*. New York: Benjamin Blom, 1964.

Index

Picture Credits

About the Author

Classical historian and literary scholar Don Nardo has written or edited numerous books about the lives, works, and characters of great English writers, among them Shakespeare, Chaucer, Dickens, Mary Shelley, and H.G. Wells. His other biographical collections include *Leaders of Ancient Greece, Rulers of Ancient Rome,* and *Women Leaders of Nations.* Mr. Nardo lives with his wife, Christine, in Massachusetts.